AUTOBIOGRAPHIES
OF CONVERSION

Joseph H. Fichter

AUTOBIOGRAPHIES
OF CONVERSION

Joseph H. Fichter

Studies in Religion and Society
Volume 17

The Edwin Mellen Press
Lewiston/Queenston

Library of Congress Cataloging-in-Publication Data

Autobiographies of conversion.

    (Studies in religion and society ; v. 17)
    Bibliography: p.
    Includes index.
    1. Unificationists--Biography 2. Conversion--Case
studies. I. Fichter, Joseph Henry, 1908-
II. Series: Studies in religion and society (New York,
N.Y.) ; v. 17.
BX9750.S48A17 1987   248.2'4 [B]   87-1634
ISBN 0-88946-857-5 (alk. paper)

This is volume 17 in the continuing series
Studies in Religion and Society
Volume 17 ISBN 0-88946-857-5
SRS Series ISBN 0-88946-863-X

The Edwin Mellen Press   The Edwin Mellen Press
Box 450   Box 67
Lewiston, New York   Queenston, Ontario
USA 14092   L0S 1L0 CANADA

Printed in the United States of America

To Young Oon Kim—Pioneer

TABLE OF CONTENTS

AUTOBIOGRAPHIES
OF CONVERSION

Joseph H. Fichter

INTRODUCTION

THE CONVERSION EXPERIENCE

The autobiographical statements of the eighteen Unificationists in this book are personal and specific, and they cannot be generalized as the typical Unification mode of conversion and recruitment. John Lofland refashioned the data from only fifteen members of the original group on the West Coast into a plausible "theory," which has gained solemn credence by a generation of sociologists. Out of this original research there emerged a "theory of conversion to a deviant perspective." This theory has been criticized by many sociologists, but it is still being employed as an explanatory scheme for recruitment to cults.[1] There is no intention here to "test" the Lofland theory with new data or to replace it with a different interpretation of biographical materials. We simply asked these Moonies for a straightforward account of their experiences.

Our only criterion for the selection of these eighteen converts to the Unification Church was their availability and willingness to tell their story to a tape recorder. We let them speak for themselves, and in each instance they were simply answering the question: "How did you happen to become a Moonie?" Gordon Alport once remarked that "if you want to know why people behave the way they do, why not just ask them?" This direct and simple approach avoids the cumbersome theories of psychological deprivation, cultural deficits, predisposing characteristics, demographic backgrounds, and situational factors. Some, or all, of these "explanations" are probably present among these

recruits who have much in common. Behavioral scientists
are always searching for repetitive patterns and
categories that help to make sense of group activities.[2]
Yet, each of these persons reveals also a unique life
experience that evolved in its own distinctive way.

Although the Unified Family is now said to contain
proportionately more males than females (quite the
opposite of conventional mainline Christian churches)
the members presented here are balanced by gender, nine
women and nine men. Except for two women recruits, who
were slightly older, all of them were in their twenties
when they met and joined the Church. They are not all
native Americans, although all have lived and worked
from time to time in the United States. They include
three Germans, two British, one French person, and one
South African. By this time, all have been matched to
their spouses by Reverend Moon and married, the earliest
in 1970 in Korea, and the most recent at Madison Square
Garden in New York in 1982.

These converts are telling their own stories
firsthand, and they are recalling events that occurred
in the last ten to fifteen years. Since they are loyal
members of the Church we may expect them to speak quite
favorably about the Moonies. We assume that their
memories are reliable and that they have no reason to
give false testimony. Nevertheless, like everyone else,
their perceptions must have been influenced by their new
affiliations.[3] It is likely that in some ways older
memories are overlaid by more recent events. For
instance, their responses concerning earlier religious
beliefs may be filtered through doctrines accepted at a
later date. When they say "I always did wonder about

the divinity of Christ," or "I never really understood the doctrine of Original Sin," are their present reflections about these central doctrines colored by their frequent discussion in lectures on the Divine Principle? One may reasonably suspect, therefore, that in some instances such theological reasons for embracing the Unification faith may have been "discovered" only after indoctrination in the movement.

For the most part, these young people came from families that had some link to organized religion, even if one or the other parent was not an active church-goer. In thirteen instances the prospective recruits had stopped going to church, usually while they were still teenagers in high school. In other words, the common pattern of conversion among them was not a "change of affiliation" from one church to another, as Ruth Wallace discusses it.[4] When they met the Moonies they had long since broken off their church affiliation; but there were five exceptions. These were Catholics who were still regular churchgoers when they began to investigate the beliefs and practices of this new religious movement. Their tendency was to proclaim that they did not shift from one belief system to another, but that they now have a better comprehension of the Christian doctrine they had always professed. In other words, they accept Reverend Moon's revelations as a fulfillment of Catholic beliefs.

What were the circumstances under which they first made contact with the Unified Family? Given the widespread allegations of enticement, seduction or entrapment of potential members to the Unification Church, it is interesting that six of these individuals say that they themselves personally sought out the Church. They learned about it in a campus newspaper ad, in a leaflet picked up on the street, in a poster attached to a telephone pole. One was attracted to a campus performance by the New Hope Singers; another saw a TV program that attacked the cults, and decided to investigate. Another was alerted to the movement by a non-member. Five of them were invited to join the Church by close friends or relatives who were already members. In the remaining cases (seven persons) the initial contact was made in the typical fashion of witnessing; that is, they were accosted by a Moonie, a total stranger, who asked them the usual questions about God, religion and the meaning of life, and invited them to visit the center.

It is almost universal in the anti-cult literature that the convert is treated as a victim who has been deliberately manipulated into membership.[5] The behavioral scientists too tend to suggest that conversion is something that is done to the individual who is passively changed by certain external factors. I have said elsewhere that we must look upon conversion as an active process; that we must take seriously the young people who say that they are on a search for the transcendent. Theirs is a religious experience that cannot be described adequately in psychological or sociological terms. "These young people are claiming that religion is precisely what it appears to be: a probing relationship in search of truth, transcendence, and the sacred. To commune with the infinite, to be in the presence of God, to experience the transcendent." This is the essence of religious conversion.[6]

Every one of our authors reports at least one spiritual experience, a vision, a dream, a war, glow of feeling, in the presence of transcendence. This had been the case also with the fifteen Moonies who told their stories in a 1978 dialogue between Evangelicals and Unificationist seminarians. They were answering the same question we addressed to our autobiographers. They told what they had found attractive in this new youth movement, and why they decided to join. In every instance they had a kind of spiritual awakening as their personal religious conversion, and also a group experience of friendliness among the people with whom they decided to associate.[7]

In some instances this spiritual experience constituted the "turning point" of which Lofland wrote, a kind of breakthrough to full acceptance of the Church. Eugenia reported, "I was quietly sitting there when I felt a tremendous wave of warmth and peace coming through me. I blanked out the man and his lecture, and I was thoroughly involved in the physical and psychological experience I was going through. I remember thinking to myself, 'this must be right.'" Joan was another who had a special awakening: "when they talked about the chapter on the Fall of Man, I suddenly felt relieved of the terrible burden of sin that I had been carrying since I lost the faith. I really felt then that the power of the Principle was acting as a purification process on my soul. I knew that something special was taking place."

One must make a logical distinction between spiritual conversion and deliberate affiliation with a church. Some believers who claim to have "found God" do not go to church and have no use for institutional religion. There are probably many regular churchgoers who have not had a spiritual awakening. In the confessional literature about religious experiences the person who is "saved" or "born-again," or converted, usually also joins a church. TV evangelists counsel their audience to affiliate with a church, or to return to the church they have been neglecting. The Moonies who witness to strangers on the street are evangelizing them, that is, giving them the good news of salvation which anticipates a spiritual awakening. In most instances, then, the conversion process of the individual is integrally related to the recruitment practices of the Church.

The story of a sophisticated college professor, who is now the American president of the Unification Church, reveals the double aspect of personal conversion and group affiliation. What is most attractive to him in the Unification movement? "Certainly, the quality of serious and genuine commitment to spiritual ideals is a central part of what moved me. Further, to experience a community of people who seek together to realize these ideals is extraordinary, uplifing and totally nourishing." Yet, there was something else that was very personal and unique. "My conversion was not startling; no outward miracle took place. Just as God finally reached Augustine while he was reading the Epistles of Paul, He reached me while I was praying with my new brothers and sisters. In my own home, in the midst of a simple prayer service similar to many others in which I had engaged, I was powerfully shaken to the foundations of my being."[8]

William James, for whom religion was a private spiritual experience, is a principal referent for people interested in the phenomenon of religious conversion. He spoke of religious conversion as an inner happening, "a process, gradual or sudden, by which a self hitherto divided and consciously wrong, inferior and unhappy, becomes unified and consciously right, superior and happy, in consequence of its firmer hold upon religious realities."[9] The secular social scientist proposes that a conversion to a cult like the Moonies is really a switch from a normal world view, about which we can all agree, to a deviant and unreal perspective.[10] The religionists will say more simply that conversion is a "turning to God." However one interprets this religious experience, one must at least say that "something happened" that caused a change in the belief and behavior of these individuals.

They changed from seekers to finders. They all became active and dedicated members of the Unified Family. As a result of taking a firmer hold upon "religious realities" they supplied what was missing in their previous "unhappy and inferior" state of soul. The substance of these religious realities lies in a book, a community and a man. The book is the sacred scripture contained in the Divine Principle.[11] The community is the fellowship extended by dedicated and concerned sisters and brothers. The man is Father Moon, the charismatic founder and prophet of the Unification movement.

Every prospective recruit is immediately confronted with the content of the book. This is the basis of the lectures to which everyone is invited. It is the theological creed, the belief system to which all members are expected to adhere. The converts in our essays differ considerably in the time they took to accept this Unification theology. Margaret struggled with it for over a year. "Perhaps I am a slow learner and maybe I am very cautious. I actually took more than a year to study and question and discuss these teachings. . . It was a time of real struggle, and on some days I believed and on other days I did not." This is in contrast with Rhinehart who said he listened to their explanation of the Divine Principle for about three hours and did not understand much of it. "I went home by subway, but I didn't remember anything of what they said. The next day I went back to learn more about their teachings, and the third day I actually joined the movement."

The converts differ also in the extent to which they accept the doctrines of Divine Principle.[12] One hesitant recruit remarked, "I thought some of its theories were more psychological than theological, but I came to see that Divine Principle had a kind of inner logic. As an Episcopalian I could agree with the ideas in it which seemed to me to be basic Christianity with an added dimension." Walter talked about a membership form which asked "when did you accept the teachings of the Divine Principle?" He did not answer because he was not sure. "I've never been asked since then whether I accept all the Principle. Obviously I accept a good deal of it, or I wouldn't have stuck it out this long." Andrew confessed that "some parts of the Principle remained questionable to me, but I think I accepted about eighty percent of it."

The content of the sacred scriptures comes from the man for whom all members hold filial devotion. Personal contact with Reverend Moon was most frequent with the neophytes who studied at the Unification seminary, but in all cases knowledge of the Divine Principle preceded contact with the leader. Belief in his messiahship is not universal among the members. "I had the impression that they didn't want to claim too much for him," said Mark. "I have since decided very definitely that he is the Messiah. That's my own personal belief. There are people who have been in the Church three or four years who won't say that. They don't know whether to believe it or not, but for myself it's true." This doctrine was not easy for everyone to accept. After hearing an older sister calmly state that Reverend Moon is the Messiah, Edward said, "I felt my spirit in shock. I was astonished. Something happened to me that is hard to describe. . . I said to myself, "I can't handle this right now - this idea of the Messiah living now on earth.'"

When Reverend Moon made his several speaking tours across the nation he provided the opportunity for members to meet and hear him in different cities. Several remarked about his "peculiar" speaking style, his loud rough voice, and the "karate-like" gestures he used. The most solemn, and joyous, communication they had with him was on the occasion of their matching to the spouse he chose for them. This seems to have been the most significant sign of their total confidence that he is indeed the messenger of God, guiding them to their marital and family destiny. They have faith in him and in his teachings of salvation and restoration.

Before the potential converts could hear the doctrine or meet the prophet they were introduced to both by the dedicated members of the Church. From the chronological perspective, therefore, the main reason why these people were first attracted to the Church was the warm, friendly attitude of the members who showed genuine affection for the newcomer. This was already noted by Lofland in the very beginning. "Lee had a particularly warm style. She greeted prospects with broad smiles and gentle bows and continually initiated conversations with them. While inquiring into matters of background and current well-being, she projected an impression of genuine personal concern."[13] Lofland calls this a "self-conscious affectation of affability," and says that "they pretended warm and friendly interest." None of our recruits suggests that this friendliness is a shallow pretense, or a fake enthusiasm, used simply as a lure that vanished once the prospect was safely in the fold. One seeks in vain among these essayists for the "forced" conversion of young Moonies.[14]

The character and the quality of the community members went deeper than a demonstration of friendliness. This was the spiritual and prayerful behavior on the part of the members. "They always prayed over the dinner," says Gertrude, "and that was my first experience of people praying with each other and out loud. Certainly I never had that in my own family at home." The encounter with piety and religiosity was almost a startling experience for young people living in a materialistic culture where prayer is either neglected or reserved for complete privacy. One gets the impression from these essays that a prayerful reference to God, or an open display of affection, is a scarce quality in contemporary society, or at least among the youths with whom they had previously associated.

Do we now have sufficient information from these eighteen Moonies to constitute a plausible theory of conversion to the Unification Church? Each person traveled a different path to the Unified Family, but it seems clear that the substance of their conversion, the "religious realities" of their commitment to the Church, emerged from their contact with the book, the man and the community. Nevertheless, there has to be something more than this to the conversion experience. Hundreds of other young people had this triple contact and did not become recruits to the Church. If we must find a central factor it has to be the one that social scientists always omit from their theories of conversion.[15] This is the ineluctable confrontation with God, the transcendent Father of creation and salvation. Without this experience there is no religious conversion. It is the universal factor of conversion, but it is not directly researchable by the tools that social scientists bring to the study of religion. Yet, to exclude it renders the whole discussion of religion fatuous.

ENDNOTES

[1]John Lofland, <u>Doomsday</u> <u>Cult</u>: A <u>Study</u> <u>of</u>
<u>Conversion</u>, <u>Proselytization</u>, <u>and</u> <u>Maintenance</u> <u>of</u> <u>Faith</u>,
Englewood Cliffs, Prentice Hall, 1977, second edition.
See also John Lofland and Rodney Stark, "Becoming A
World-saver: A Theory of Conversion to A Deviant
Perspective," <u>American</u> <u>Sociological</u> <u>Review</u>, 1965, vol.
39, pp. 862-874.

[2]The most useful discussion of the religious
conversion process is presented by James T. Richardson,
Mary White Stewart and Robert B. Simmonds, <u>Organized</u>
<u>Miracles</u>, New Brunswick, Transaction, 1979, pp. 231-274,
"Conversion Models."

[3]This point is made by James A. Beckford,
"Accounting for Conversion," <u>British</u> <u>Journal</u> <u>of</u>
<u>Sociology</u>, 1978, 29, 249-262, and also by B. Taylor,
"Recollection and Membership: Converts' Talk and the
Ratiocination of Commonality," <u>Sociology</u>, 1978, 12, 316-
324.

[4]Ruth Wallace, "A Model of Change of Religious
Affiliation," <u>Journal</u> <u>for</u> <u>the</u> <u>Scientific</u> <u>Study</u> <u>of</u>
<u>Religion</u>, 1975, vol. 14, pp. 345-355, who hypothesizes
four cultural "deficits" as conditions for change. See
also Frank Newport, "The Religious Switcher in the
United States," <u>American</u> <u>Sociological</u> <u>Review</u>, August,
1979, pp. 528-552.

[5]The most useful discussion of anti-cultists is by
Anson Shupe and David Bromley, <u>The</u> <u>New</u> <u>Vigilantes</u>:
<u>Deprogrammers</u>, <u>Anti-Cultists</u> <u>and</u> <u>the</u> <u>New</u> <u>Religions</u>,
Beverly Hills, Sage, 1980.

[6]Joseph H. Fichter, "Youth in Search of the
Sacred," pp. 21-41, in Bryan Wilson, ed., <u>The</u> <u>Social</u>
<u>Impact</u> <u>of</u> <u>New</u> <u>Religious</u> <u>Movements</u>, New York, Rose of
Sharon Press, 1981.

[7]See Richard Quebedeaux and Rodney Sawatsky, eds., Evangelical-Unification Dialogue, New York, Rose of Sharon Press, 1979, "Testimonies," pp. 1-76.

[8]Mose Durst, To Bigotry, No Sanction: Reverend Sun Myung Moon and the Unification Church, Chicago, Regnery, 1984, pp. 35, 40.

[9]William James, Varieties of Religious Experience, New York, Longmans Green, 1912, p. 189.

[10]John Lofland, op. cit., p. 1.

[11]According to Sang Hun Lee, President of the Unification Thought Institute, the Korean title is more correctly translated as Unification Principle.

[12]The Unification creed was formulated in a dozen theological statements of faith professed by the Barrytown seminarians in 1976. See Frederick Sontag, Sun Myung Moon and the Unification Church, Nashville, Abingdon, 1977, pp. 102-105.

[13]Doomsday Cult, p. 175.

[14]See the excellent analysis of this allegation by Thomas Robbins, "Constructing the Cultist Mind Control," Sociological Analysis, Fall, 1984, vol. 45, pp. 241-256.

[15]This central factor is omitted also from the "new" reconception discussed by Theodore Long and Jeffrey Hadden, "Religious Conversion and the Concept of Socialization," Journal for the Scientific Study of Religion, March, 1983, vol. 22, 1, pp. 1-14.

BEATRICE — AMERICAN PIONEER

The most dramatic spiritual experience I ever had was on a visit to some friends at Stanford University. I was sitting there writing in my journal when suddenly I felt that I was moved outside of my room, standing at a point where I could see the whole earth covered with gloom and despair. There were cities that looked like they had been burned in a fire. The buildings stood like skeletons. There was no living thing, no grass, no trees, no animals. Through the darkness I saw bits of light in different places that seemed to symbolize hope. All of a sudden a much bigger light burst across the sky at San Francisco. Then a strange voice spoke to me from deep within my self. It told me "you must go to San Francisco; and it's there that you will begin your work."

All this happened in 1961 when I was taking some time off to recoup my finances so I could return and finish my degree. If San Francisco held the solution to my problems it wasn't going to be easy because I was living at home in Washington State at the time. I had had other spiritual experiences in my life. I had also been studying philosophy to understand these experiences and how to deal with my questions about the meaning of life. I was always open to people with new spiritual ideas, and I had a strong intuition that some leader was about to appear who would coordinate people like myself, who wanted to do something about human suffering and the terrible state of the world.

Eventually I managed to reach San Francisco, where I got a part-time job to support myself while I was living in Berkeley and taking courses at the University. The vision I had made me alert to look for whatever it was that I was supposed to do, but I was there almost two years before I bumped into the church. I saw an ad in the student newspaper that said, "Christ has returned and is now on earth. Within a short time we will experience a great crisis, and the purpose is to turn people back to God." Naturally I thought this was some crazy group, but then I thought how can I afford not to check them out. So I went to the address which was a small apartment over a Chinese restaurant. I soon found that it was a kind of transient place. Peter Koch had just left for Germany; Young Oon Kim lived in San Francisco with some of the older members of the Church. Edwin Ang introduced me to the Unified Family - as they called themselves - and instructed me in the teachings of <u>Divine</u> <u>Principle</u>.

In those days we didn't have plans for establishing centers and forming communities. We just thought that communal living was a very practical thing to do. That way everybody could live together, and they pooled the money they made on their jobs. It wasn't part of a consolidated conversion process with seminars and lectures and workshops. No one urged me to move in. I didn't ask anybody. I just assumed that I should do so because I wanted to be part of the group. New members were being constantly attracted, and they had the same desire to live communally. We were growing fast and we soon had to move form the apartment to a much larger and more convenient residence.

In the new house we kept a fairly equal balance of girls and boys, but for many years the Unified Family had more women joining than men. I think that in the sixties women saw a real avenue for self-expression in this movement and for doing something concrete with their lives. You really felt that you could pour your whole life into something very substantial, where you didn't have limits placed on your talents and aspirations. On the other hand, maybe men were scared off when they saw these efficient women running things. It was very hard for men at that time. I can recall rather concretely the extreme difficulties that some men had when they did join because the leaders were women. They felt very threatened by that, even outspokenly so, and some of them just simply couldn't stand it. It must have been hard for them because we were all experimenting with organization and procedures. The first missionaries from Korea were women, and Reverend Moon himself didn't arrive in the States until 1965. Even that was just for a visit, and he didn't come to stay until 1972.

Now it is definitely the opposite in the Unification Church, where the men have a great deal more opportunity than the women. Both the brothers and the sisters were serious people and there was no fooling around. The community itself was attractive because it was a haven from all the worries and distractions of the world. Everyone was very serious and we had mutual respect because of that. There was a very deep feeling of family love that superceded romantic love. You

needed a community of like-minded persons if you were
going to live this sacrificial life.

We didn't talk much in those days of spiritual
children and spiritual parents. If we all had a "true"
parent in the Church in that area I suppose it would
have been Miss Kim, who was the first missionary to
America from Korea, but our center wasn't so closely
connected with hers. We would go over to San Francisco
maybe once a week, and certainly on holidays, but I did
not find her able to relate to me in the kind of
parental manner that Americans understand. I think I
also regarded my mother in those days as more of a
friend than anything else. It may have been I sought
that kind of relationship with Miss Kim, who wanted
members to be subordinate to her, but I couldn't arrange
that.

I kept good contact with my two younger brothers
and with my parents. I found out quite a few years
later that my father had us investigated by the FBI, who
gave a fairly positive report on us. At least, they
couldn't find anything wrong with this movement, which
wasn't as well-known as it is now. My father told me on
the phone once that he thought they were trying to get
all my money, which was funny because I didn't have any
money. I used to try to share some of my beliefs that
were exciting to me with my mother, and she would say
"Yes, I'm sure that is so true." It was a strange
situation. They must have been somewhat concerned, but
they tried very hard to accept what I was doing.

As a matter of fact, I didn't communicate with them
- except accidentally - for about seven years. This is

not the practice today - contrary to the accusations -
but in those days we thought it was necessary to cut off
all ties with our past life, in particular our parents,
because we were going to get new parents. We didn't
think of "true parents" as applying to Reverend and Mrs
Moon. That term was not available then, but we meant
God. Jesus was our elder brother. God was our parent,
our father. We didn't hear it because maybe Miss Kim
didn't pick it up. It wasn't in the early books; that's
for sure. We prayed in the name of the Lord. We knew
that Reverend Moon was in the Messiah's position, but he
hadn't yet become the true parent. I think it was only
after the birth of his third or fourth child that this
came to be a significant teaching of the Church.

Nevertheless, the concept of the true vocation to
marriage and family had to be there from the beginning,
as an essential aspect of Unification life. When I
first heard the chapter about the Fall in the <u>Divine
Principle</u> I knew it was going to be necessary to marry,
and I asked about that. "Does everyone have to get
married?" I was willing to follow the church teaching,
but to be forced into marriage was a big stumbling block
for me. I didn't want to be pushed into something like
that, and I was sure that I could always say no. But I
had to say that if it is God's will I'll have to be
ready for it. If what they said was true, that you're
going to be perfect in your relationship with God - and
that was the most important thing to me - that it's not
going to be threatened by a marriage relationship
anyway. I would have to be open-minded and go through
with it.

My experience before I met the Church was that male-female involvements did threaten my relationship with God. I had always tried to avoid sinful actions in this regard, and I have to say that my conversion to the Unified Family was not a discovery of virtue and religion and God. My family was only mildly religious. We went to any convenient church in the neighborhood. My mother studied Rosicrucianism for many years, and was more religious than my father. It was a strange combination. We always went to Sunday school, and I prayed and believed in God. When I joined the Church I realized that sex relations would not be a problem. We thought we had entered the Garden of Eden because the atmosphere was so totally changed. We didn't feel sexual temptation. It wasn't something we had to fight off all the time. Our communal life was very natural and human and a real help to lead a pure life.

The Church was growing on the West Coast in the mid- sixties, and Dora Zorn had established a fairly good-size center in Los Angeles. I went down to visit her several times and liked what she was doing. She and the other leaders felt it was time to do pioneering work in Florida where the Church then had no members. I was assigned to pray about the best location in the State and then go there. Based on my prayer I decided not to go to Miami because it seemed too touristy, and I thought I would meet more serious and more substantial people in Tampa. I arrived at the Tampa bus station with thirteen dollars in my pocket. I bought a news-paper to look for a room to rent, and I bought a map of the city so I could find the address. After I paid for the room I think I had two dollars left. There was no air conditioning then. It was a very poor place with cockroaches, and I had never seen a cockroach before.

In those days we all had to work and make income. So the first thing was to get a job and then in the time off from the job to do some witnessing. I was not trained for typing, but I used to take temporary jobs and learned how to do everything secretarial on the job. So that was beneficial too, and since it was temporary I changed jobs a lot. At first I tried witnessing to people I worked with, but that was usually a disaster because they just assumed you were very weird. I guess there is no place for religion in a business office. They say religion and politics don't mix, and it looks also as if religion and business don't mix. No one had heard of the Unified Family in Florida; there weren't any Jesus groups around like out on the Coast; and the new-age mentality hadn't arrived yet. So I probably just seemed a little bizarre to those people.

I might have looked a little bizarre too because I was anything but modishly dressed in those days. The early American members were almost Puritanical in some ways. We had the idea that you don't waste energy on anything that isn't in the religious mainstream. Even walking down the street I always kept my eyes straight ahead and never looked in store windows. Satan and his spirits were everywhere to tempt us in our divine mission. So I didn't even know what the fashion was. But I did not avoid people on the street. I had learned the friendly techniques of witnessing, contacting young people at lunch-time and after work in the early evening. There were a lot of elderly retired people in Tampa and in nearby St. Petersburg, where I used to sit

on the park benches and talk with them about God. I
never asked anybody for money. The practice of
fundraising had not yet been introduced.

It looked as though Washington would be the logical
American headquarters for the Church. Miss Kim
pioneered in England in 1965 but returned the next year
to join Colonel Pak at the Washington center. Then she
invited me to take over the secretarial work. Up to
that point we had no brochures or flyers to give to
prospective members or just to publicize our movement.
I designed the first witnessing literature and did the
very first publications we ever had. We thought it
would be useful to distribute a kind of newsletter, and
I was responsible for that. I learned a lot from that,
just by doing it. Some of the people who came in later
were professionals in this kind of work,and they took
over to produce the excellent publications that the
movement now distributes.

What I liked better, and was more experienced, was
witnessing on the streets of Washington and teaching
new members how to witness. For many years I brought
more people to the Church than anyone else. I really
believed that the Divine Principle had an extremely
important message for people and was valuable to every
individual person. I did a lot of lecturing at the
center. After I would bring somebody all the way
through the Principle I would take them right out and
witness with them. Most of the witnessing I did was
when I took these members out and tried to show them how
to do it. I was never good at the aggressive approach
and didn't come on strong. I tried to be friendly and
had a strong feeling of responsibility for others. I

was very honest and sincere with those new members, and we still continue to be very close friends. In fact, I married one of them.

It was only later that we talked about having spiritual children. This concept came in with the influx of Japanese members who use it very much and consider it extremely important. We are, of course, a spiritual family and it is meaningful to think of ourselves this way, but I have always resisted the notion that the people I brought into the Church are my spiritual children. I don't like to think of them as children, or that I had to help raise them. I always thought of it as helping them to grow. It was always very important to maintain respect for them and receive it from them. I feel that that's the essential ingredient in love. If we have any trouble in the Church between men and women it seems to be only in cases where they don't have enough respect for one another.

Genuine love among us is always accompanied by - and is founded upon - genuine respect. That's another thing Reverend Moon says, even when he talks about the dominion of the husband in marriage, or even Abel's dominion over Cain. He says it is the dominion of love, but I think we have to be mature enough to understand that the husband's conjugal love does not mean control over the wife. There is a lot of talk in the Church about our adoption of the Confucian family system, where the females are supposed to be subject to the males. You don't have to be a women's liberationist to appreciate that that doesn't work in the practical everyday American life of married Moonies.

Reverend Moon had planned to do a matching and a blessing when he first visited here in 1965, but nothing was ready so he called it off. Then when he came in 1969 he did the first blessing in America, which was for thirteen couples. Early the next year Miss Kim went to Korea where she learned that Reverend Moon was planning to have a big wedding in October. She wrote back to Farley Jones, who was president of the American church at the time, and said that Reverend Moon wanted to include some American couples. Those of us who felt we were ready for marriage were asked to send photographs so that a matching could be made of the pictures, even though we didn't know who was going to marry whom. That was decided by Reverend Moon, who invited us to Seoul for the holy wine ceremony followed by the big wedding. We were seven American couples in the total of 777 couples married there in 1970.

We visited there for a while, in Japan as well as in Korea, and were introduced to many of the Oriental members. For most of us it was the first time we experienced a kind of denigration of our own culture. Even Miss Kim, who was back in her own culture, seemed to release a lot of her pent-up feelings about Americans. Here we were in this very vulnerable state, about to be married to people whom we had never thought of marrying, and we were subject to this criticism. Fortunately their speeches were minimally translated. It seems that the Japanese did not think we were genuine Unificationists because we didn't do fundraising. We were supporting the Church by contributing the wages and salaries we made. I really believe we did as much witnessing as they did, but we did it on our extra time.

This was not my first brush with a foreign culture. I was an exchange student in Europe when I was sixteen,and I experienced the same kind of cultural myopia in the family I lived with in Denmark. They were so immersed in their own culture that they thought everything I did as being crazy and stupid. We managed to survive the Oriental criticisms, and we agreed to follow their custom of postponing the consummation of our marriages. When we came back we agreed that, in addition to the forty-day separation of indemnity, we would not have children for three years. But almost everybody broke that agreement. We were all getting older.

It is an Oriental notion in our Church that you should have large families. There is also the idea that Adam and Eve were given the responsibility to populate the earth. I think most Korean families are very big. That may be in the culture as well as in the religion, but the sex of the child is important. If you talk to a traditional, conservative Japanese man you get the impression that girl babies aren't real babies. There is also an attitude in the Church that if you have daughters it means that the wife is still dominant in the relationship, which isn't supposed to be the right way. When you have a son it shows that the husband has become dominant in the relationship. So there is a great deal of pressure on the wives to have lots of children, and preferably sons. There is a tendency in the American church to have what in today's America would be considered a pretty good-size family, maybe four or five children. I didn't care so much for child- ren before I was married, but now that we have a boy and a girl I love them very much. I think we all seem to feel that way once we have our own children.

We are all dedicated to the ideal of the God-centered family as well as the interracial and international unification of all God's children. Some of the members talk about the Koreanization of the movement, but I recognize an even stronger Japanese influence. The Church had grown rapidly in Japan, even before Reverend Moon's marriage in 1960. The members were persecuted by the Communists, but they developed a strong solidarity and a sense of mission. When they came here they told us they were the mother country, the Eve country, while America is the Archangel (Lucifer) country. They must educate and restore the Archangel, and they thought they were supposed to teach us how to live the Principle.

Reverend Moon seems to have a special love of the Japanese members because they are hardworking and obedient. They were the ones who introduced street begging and fundraising to the American scene. I think there is sometimes ill-feeling by the Korean members against the Japanese. I am sure it was partly because of the Japanese occupation and long domination of Korea and the fact that Koreans living in Japan still suffer prejudice and discrimination as an ethnic minority. We westerners think of interracial and inter-ethnic harmony in terms of Orientals and Caucasians, but we forget the ancient antagonisms among Chinese, Japanese, Koreans, and other nations of the East.

Reverend Moon continually teaches that everybody is equal to everybody else, and that's across gender lines too. We are God's Unified Family. I think the Divine

<u>Principle</u> itself, certainly the way we interpreted it in the early days, was almost liberationist because it taught that men were not sufficient by themselves. If women weren't, neither were men. Women and men need each other in order to be the proper object of God's love and attention. It was taken for granted that a balance could be achieved and that this would be based on the combination of individuals. In some situations the wife would be dominant, and properly so. When the Japanese Moonies came here they put the emphasis in the other direction, as though it is really important that men be dominant both in the family and in the church leadership. In the practicality of American marriages and American church relationships, these contradictions tend to be resolved. You understand what you are supposed to do and what you can do.

II

CHARLES — CATHOLIC SEMINARIAN

In the summer of 1968 I met a Unificationist at a
Catholic charismatic weekend retreat given under the
direction of Francis MacNutt and Dolores Fassbinder. I
was a second-year seminarian at the Cardinal Glennon
College, which is part of Kenrick Seminary in St. Louis.
In that summer we were trying to respond basically to
Vatican II's request for better priestly formation. We
spent most of a six-weeks summer course studying the
Council's document, Optatam Totius, the Decree on
Priestly Formation, and during the last week of the
program these two Catholic Pentecostals came to inspire
us. It was my first contact with the charismatics, and
I was intrigued with the novelty of their approach.

During the prayer meeting on the last evening a
woman asked us to pray for her husband, who was unhappy
and sad and depressed. This was new to me. I had never
experienced the charismatic way of open prayer and group
worship. After the meeting I went up to the woman and
expressed my concern about her husband. We talked for
almost two hours, mainly about prayer. She said things
about the spirit world and about Satan I hadn't heard
before. My seminary background didn't prepare me for
people who still actually believed in that kind of
stuff. I was just very curious.

She invited me to hear more about it and gave me
her address where I visited her the following Wednesday.

She read to me from an outline she had made of Young Oon Kim's book, The Divine Principle and its Application. A few days later she read the second chapter, the lecture on the Fall of Man. I found it very stimulating and was eager to hear more, so I went back several times in the next two weeks and heard the teaching on through the mission of Jesus. Her husband had come back to St. Louis, and they were preparing to return to Washington, so they hurried me through the rest of the teaching. I got a four-hour testimony from her husband, who told me about levitating when he was a child. He spoke of spiritual experiences that were very foreign to me. This couple seemed perfectly normal people to me, and I felt I should investigate further.

In September I went back for my third year in the seminary. I made a deal with God to help me discover whether what these people were telling me was the truth. I knew I could be mistaken one way or the other. My intuition was that there may be some new truth here. My deal with God was: "If this is wrong please let me know within the next semester, but if everything points to validating this new experience then I will leave the seminary at the end of the semester." I had a consider-able investment in my years of study for the priesthood, and I was not consciously looking to leave the seminary. Yet I felt there was something missing in my training for the priesthood. During lectures in the seminary I would hear things that sounded so much like what the Principle was saying. I never thought of this involve-ment with the Unified Family as a rejection of my Catholic faith. If I had to figure that I was renounc-ing the faith then I would have been very suspicious of my motives.

I prayed a lot about it; I prayed the Rosary every day. I did not expect spiritual experiences; in fact, I would have been skeptical about that and would probably have attributed it to some subconscious willing on my part. I talked with a few of the seminarians about these new ideas, but they weren't interested. Ironically, at the same time, one of my classmates locked himself in his room for the whole semester and was reading to try to decide whether or not God existed. He came to the conclusion that he just did not really believe in God. Meanwhile, I felt I was getting closer to Jesus. I felt there was an explanation within the Principle that was quite coherent about the way the world is. It gave me an effective way to develop my spiritual life, which I was not doing at all in the seminary.

Early in the Fall I gave Ms. Kim's book to the Spiritual Director and asked him to read it. I don't believe he even looked at it; at least, he didn't take me, or it, seriously. I think he felt that this would "just blow over." The seminarians didn't have much contact with the Spiritual Father, but we were supposed to meet with him at least once each semester. I think there was confusion what to do about the spirituality of the seminarians. We were right in the middle of the transition period following the Council, and we were a notoriously conservative seminary. Starting in 1965 they did make a lot of effort to change from the older regime to a newer one, but many of the people on the faculty seemed to be even more confused than the students.

Perhaps the confusion lay in their conservative way of presenting the whole system of Catholicism. As I look back I see the difference between just being told about Christology and actually experiencing Jesus. Receiving a Christology from above, as it were, where you are told that Jesus is God, that He is your Savior, that you must believe all this as the teaching of the Church, is not so immediately experiential for you. What the Divine Principle was offering was more of a Christology from below, where you try to understand and talk about Jesus' human struggles. I found this to be more personal and more persuasive than any series of theses asserting who Jesus is.

When I left the seminary in early 1969 I just told the Rector that I was interested in a different kind of ecumenical work in my life. I told him that I appreciated all that the seminary had done for me; and I was honest about that. In some respects I regretted the departure, but I was not depressed about it. I had many friends there, and I really wanted to share with them what I was experiencing; but there wasn't much interest in it, or even much sympathy for me.

It was a different story when I told my family at home, especially my mother. She is more religious than my father, who is a convert to Catholicism. My older sister is married and a good practicing Catholic; and my younger brother is a daily communicant, just the way I was. Like a lot of other people, they had considered me a model seminarian, and they were very surprised when I left the seminary. I tried to reassure them that I was doing the right thing, but there was considerable disappointment and confusion on their part.

They didn't know anything about the Unification Church, which was then called the Unified Family. Reverend Moon had not yet taken up residence in this country. The news media had not begun to attack us, so there were no slanderous stories about the so-called cults and the Moonies. But just the thought that I was discontinuing the seminary, and was doing something besides a conventional Catholic course of action, was a great puzzle to them. I could hear my mother crying late at night. She just felt very confused by the whole thing and virtually told me she was losing her mind. In certain subtle ways she seemed to be contemplating suicide. I don't believe she would ever have done that, but I think she had the feeling she was going to die.

My father was disappointed in me but was less expressive or demonstrative than my mother. They think I made the wrong choices but know that I made them with good intentions. My Dad was more ready to accept and respect my decisions, and probably hopes that someday I will change my mind. There was no way I could reassure my family, and it was a sort of relief to leave home at Easter time when a center was opened in St. Louis. Meanwhile, I was continuing my education at the University of Missouri in St. Louis, getting my Bachelor degree with a major in philosophy. At the center I was associating with four other members, taking my college courses every day, witnessing to people three or four times a week, and supporting myself with two jobs.

After a short while another group of people joined us, and I was actually teaching them the Principle. It was a very loose and informal introduction to

membership. We had a simple membership card on which
you wrote your name and address, your parents' address,
the name of the person who taught you the Divine
Principle, and the date on which you accepted the
teachings of Divine Principle. I didn't get around to
signing membership till November, 1969. We didn't do
any fundraising in those early years, but we supported
the center with our pooled incomes. I had a pretty good
paying job at United Parcel Service where I sorted mail
at night; and I also worked in a bakery on weekends.

After my graduation from the University in 1970 I
stayed in St. Louis for six months, and I continued to
hold two part-time jobs. I witnessed to newcomers,
invited people to the center and did most of the
lecturing and teaching of the Principle there. The
movement was growing with a lot of small centers
scattered around the country. Now the plan was formed
to consolidate and draw these centers back to the church
headquarters in Washington. I was called to Washington
late in the Fall of 1971 to do a Level III training
program with Phil and Vivian Burleigh who had witnessed
to me originally in St. Louis. At the end of the year
Reverend Moon arrived in America and selected seventy
pioneers to accompany him on his seven-city speaking
tour. More changes occurred in plans, and we were
shifted to New York.

We ended up at the Netherlands Avenue center in the
Bronx, where I was supposed to be a trainee in the Level
III program. They used me actually to do some of the
teaching. I don't think anyone had any real formal
education at the time in the theological, moral and
historical system of the Church. We did a lot of

reading and discussion, and the emphasis of our training was on the practical life of the Church membership. My faith and loyalty continued to grow in the Divine Principle. I believed that I had not broken with my earlier commitment as a Catholic. Because my Catholic upbringing had taught me obedience I really didn't have any other choice. I mean that I had been taught always to follow my conscience. Through my daily prayers I felt that this was God's calling for me and I had no other choice but to respond. I was not following my own desires but this was a step I was being told to take.

The fact is that when you become a member of the Church you are not asked to repudiate any of your religious beliefs as though you had rejected your previous false religion to embrace the true revelation according to Mr. Moon. What happens is an inner change of your relationship with God. I guess you have to call it a religious conversion away from your earlier nonreflective automatic prayer life to a very positive communication with the loving Father of all creation. That's why I don't think I gave up the Catholic Church when I became a Unificationist. I live all my Catholic beliefs more intensely now and with a greater awareness of their meaning.

The training program in New York was interrupted when the word went out that the church needed money to buy the Belvedere Estate in Tarrytown. At this point everybody began to do fundraising, and we became mendicants like the medieval monks. This was my first experience of going up to people and asking them for money. The candles we offered people were made at the center in College Park near Washington and shipped to us in New York. I was on the very first Mobile team sent out to fundraise from the New York center. At the same time I was working for an insurance agency down on John Street in the Wall Street area, and I would come home every evening and sell candles. I was never good at selling on the streets, but I did quite well door to door and did a lot of selling in the residential areas of Queens.

That was in 1972 when hardly anybody knew anything about the Unification Church and Reverend Moon had not yet become a public figure. Sometimes you ran into people who were anti-religious, but I was not rejected specifically because I was a Unificationist. We were not yet called "Moonies," and even the most fundamentalist of Christians knew nothing about our Church. So it was not hard at all to fundraise when I told people that I was with a Christian group interested in family development and better home life. I told them we had a lecture program and needed money to rent places to give those lectures.

Fundraising around the country was successful enough to purchase the Belvedere Estate at Tarrytown, which we used as an international training center. All kinds of teams came over from Europe to start what they called the 100-day training program. It was a stiff regime of lectures on the Divine Principle, speeches from Reverend Moon, discussions with Young We Kim who was president of the movement in Korea. This was the first time the Unification Church was presented as a logical religious movement in the way that most people hear about it now. I was close to this whole development because for the first five months I had the management, or caretaking, of the whole plant at Belvedere.

This appointment at Belvedere gave me the opportunity to know Reverend Moon at close range. In my experiences before 1973 my spiritual focus was on the teachings of the <u>Divine</u> <u>Principle</u>, with hardly any reference to the founder of the movement. His presence in America made a significant difference not only for me but for the whole church. There was a big transition for the American membership, and many of them didn't make it. They just didn't like things to change from the way they had been. It has to be admitted that there is considerable cultural dissidence between the American mentality and the Korean mentality, which I take to be a basic and important aspect of restoration. Some people get frustrated because they feel the Church is too Korea-oriented.

Mr. Moon's speaking tours in 1973 drew a lot of attention and the beginning of unfavorable public criticism, but it also had a double effect on the membership of the Church. On the one hand, we gained a large number of new people, but there were also too many of the older members dropping out. I think some of them left because the expected restoration was not emerging right before their eyes. They had joined with a certain hope and didn't realize how long it would take. They found themselves unhappy because they wanted something more immediate. Another fact is that it is not easy to be a Moonie. We work hard and pray a lot, and we fast regularly. I have done several seven-day fasts and about thirty three-day fasts, and actually it is not difficult for me.

At the end of 1973 my mission was changed from New York to California, where I was designated the leader for the southern part of the State, and where I chanced one evening to meet Rosemary who was destined to be my wife. I was pretty much in charge there for a year and a half, while Reverend Moon made two nation-wide speaking tours. The leaders of the International One World Crusade were then distributed around the country, and a team of almost fifty German members came to live and work and witness in California. Paul Werner was the only IOWC commander who kept intact his team's nationality. All the other commanders had mixed groups of Europeans. That was also the year when large numbers of Japanese members began to come to the States.

By this time I had been long enough in the movement to be eligible for matching and the Blessing. We had heard rumors in the latter half of 1974 that a matching was about to take place, and this rumor was confirmed in January of 1975 when invitations were issued by Reverend Moon to about 150 American members. We were all on the plane together flying to Korea, none of us knowing who our spouse would be, or even whether we would be matched. Reverend Moon began the matching on the afternoon of the first day; we practiced for the public ceremony the next day, and on the third day we were part of the large blessing of 1,800 couples in the large auditorium at Seoul. Of course, this was not a legally recognized marriage because the officals could not issue a marriage license for non-Korean citizens.

When we returned to New York we were married civilly and then separated to follow individual missions for the church. My wife was born in Pittsburgh, raised and educated as a Catholic, and joined the Unified Family in San Francisco. She had been a member longer than I and was thirty-three years of age at the time of our marriage. The period of separation for most of the couples married in 1975 in Korea was three years, but we expected that an exception would be made in our case because of Rosemary's "advanced age." The fact is that ours was a 21-month separation, and we came together to begin our married life when I was a student at the Barrytown seminary.

After the wedding I returned to work at the Los Angeles Center until the spring (May) of 1975 when I was assigned to do the 120-day training program at the Barrytown Center, which had recently been purchased from the Christian Brothers. This was fairly rigorous training under Reverend Ken Sudo, even for those of us who had been working in the church for some years. There were two months of intense lecturing, discussion and lecture practice, followed by sixty days of witness- ing and fundraising outside the area of Barrytown. The first class to start seminary training at Barrytown entered in September of that year, 1975, but I was sent to Lincoln, Nebraska to recruit new members and to lecture on the Principle. Since there was no center there, the experience was a typical example of pioneer- ing.

Shortly thereafter I was asked to take charge of a training center we had established just outside of Norman, Oklahoma. This constituted a series of 21-day programs of advanced lectures for new members who had already received introductory lectures. Members came from about twenty different states, went through the cycle of training and then returned to their own centers. That continued till the summer of 1976 when our education team went East to prepare for the first "God bless America" Rally at Yankee Stadium. After the campaign was over I expected to return to Oklahoma, but I was called to cooperate with the program for the Washington Monument Rally which drew over 300,000 people in September. As soon as that was completed I did start my studies at the Unification seminary.

In the fourth and last semester we were asked "who would like to go on to graduate school beyond Barrytown?" A number of us, including me, made the request, but in any case the whole graduating class was sent to England that summer for the Home Church Experience. I was in South London the whole time in charge of different teams and also lecturing on the Principle at the Unification Center there. At the end of the summer we returned to the States, and I was accepted for the graduate program in systematic theology at the Catholic University in Washington.

It was a long and winding road from my early days in a Catholic seminary to a Catholic Graduate School in Theology, and I can hardly find similarities between the two. I completed the courses leading to the Master's degree in Divinity, which opened up a much broader religious vista than I ever dreamed possible under Roman auspices. As I work in the doctoral program I appreciate the study of comparative theology that investigates the wide varieties of conceptualizations of divinity. I am most interested in methods in the study of theology, and I am confident that the Catholic University at Washington ranks with some of the better divinity schools in the country. I do not find these academic experiences a challenge to my faith in the theological system of Reverend Moon. No one is witnessing to me to alter my chosen path to God.

III

JOAN — REVELATIONS AND DREAMS

When I was sixteen I had a conversion experience in the Baptist Church. This was a well-advertised revival meeting I was attending, and when the preacher said, "Jesus will forgive you your sins," I felt a burden lift from me and a great joy and peace came to me after that. So I knew then that I was a born-again Christian, even though I wasn't a Baptist, and it wasn't completely unexpected.

The fact is that as an infant I was christened in the Anglican Church. My mother was a Methodist but not a churchgoer. She was a trained registered nurse who told me she was disillusioned with the Church because she saw clergymen refuse to minister to sick and dying patients who were not of their faith. I sensed that she was also a bit psychic because she was often contacted by Spiritualists. My father was registered as an Anglican but he studied Rosicrucianism for some time, and I don't think he was a believing Christian. They said I could be anything I wanted. From the time I was eight I attended a Catholic convent school, but went to the Anglican Sunday School where I was confirmed at age fifteen. Even in my childhood I was aware of disagreements and conflicts between the churches.

In spite of such confusion I was actually very religious-oriented as a child. I remember I used to pray every night to do God's will when I grew up. My relationship with Jesus was first of all that of a friend, my closest friend. When I was in high school I joined the Students' Christian Association who invited different speakers to come in. I remember a young woman missionary who described her own conversion experience when she accepted Jesus as her Lord. At that moment, she said, all the sins of her past life came before her. Suddenly I too became aware of the fact that we are all sinners. I had never been conscious of that before. Now I realized that I was a very guilty person because of the wrong things I had done. I felt this burden of guilt. According to her, Jesus took your sins away and forgave you, so I prayed very much to be relieved of my guilt. Shortly after that I was reborn among the Baptists.

Later when I was at the Teacher Training college I was still involved very much with the Student Christian Association. Some of us used to pray together at lunchtime, but we had no place to gather for worship. The school authorities were impressed with our efforts and determination, and they actually provided a little chapel for our use. I considered myself a devout Christian, and Jesus was always very real to me. Sometimes when I prayed with my friends I felt him like a presence in the room. I was full of peace and joy. I really prayed to be the kind of Christian who radiates a godliness so that people would know when I was in their presence.

When I finished teaching training at twenty (1960) I was offered a scholarship to a Missionary College in California. All I needed was to pay my own travel fee to America. I couldn't go straight away anyhow because

I had got a bursary and was committed to teaching for two years. Then I prayed very much about it and came to the conclusion that I did not really want to be a missionary at a South African mission station. I actually grew up on a farm in Africa where I had many contacts with missionaries, and I knew what mission stations were like. My grandfather had an estate there, and my father was manager of a sugar cane farm. He later became junior manager in a big company, and we lived in Swaziland for about eight years. While I was teaching young children I reflected over these early memories of the missionaries I had known. I still wanted to influence people to live better lives, but I decided that I could succeed in this better as a social worker than as a missionary.

At that point my father had a promotion to general manager of his company, with a good increase in salary. He offered to support me so that I could finish my studies and get a degree in social work at the University. For two years I studied in this academic program, with a heavy concentration on psychology and sociology. I studied theories of personality and explanations of human behavior that completely excluded any reference to God's existence, much less to His divine providence. My faith in God was not only shaken; it was destroyed. I was in my twenties and I discovered sex. My behavior was shameful, but I felt no shame. I had intimate relations with several men, and for a while I rationalized this as perfectly normal behavior in a secular modern society.

As a matter of fact I was no longer believing as a Christian, but I did not break my ties with organized religion. I am sure that I succeeded in concealing my worldly conduct from the church members, but I continued actively in the University as chairman of the Anglican Student Association. I organized prayer meetings and Bible study groups, but no one seemed to notice that I did not participate in them. I was a member of the National Student Committee for all South African Universities. I like to think that I was not the only one there leading a kind of double life, but the duplicity of the situation was beginning to bother me. I had no faith in God, and I wondered whether I would regain that faith under other circumstances. I had my degree in social work and was employed as a family worker when I decided to leave my job and my friends to see the world.

My sister is married to an Englishman, and through him I was offered a position working in a child guidance clinic in London. The change was good for me in the sense that I could now deal with new people under different circumstances. My training in psychology helped me to apply humanistic reasoning to the process of child maturation. The truly mature person is one who can relate completely to other people, and it was only later that I recognized the connection between maturity and spirituality, and came to conclude that Jesus was the only person who was truly mature. I was not yet ready to return to such religious philosophy of human relations, but I suppose that God was at this time preparing me for my return to him.

On my first holiday I went to Italy and visited the various places associated with the history of Christian civilization. I was also interested in architecture and painting, in opera and ballet. I spent too much money

and was low on funds, so I went to the American Episcopal Church and asked if they could put me up for three
days before I went back to England. The minister himself happened to be away on holiday, so on the third day
I handed my keys to the church secretary who was an
American. I told him that I did not feel the presence
of God in that church; he replied that he felt exactly
the same.

Here is another turning point in my life. He and
his wife were members of a group they called the Unified
Family and were on a kind of sabbatical in Rome, he
studying opera and she studying art. I spent several
hours at their home that afternoon while they explained
this new philosophy to me. It seems to me that the
spiritual relationship they had with Sun Myung Moon was
much stronger and more intimate than the relationship I
had had with Jesus in my adolescent years. They read
from their book, the <u>Divine</u> <u>Principle</u>, and when they
talked about chapter two on the Fall of Man, I suddenly
felt relieved of the terrible burden of sin that I had
been carrying since I lost my faith. I really felt then
that the power of the <u>Principle</u> was acting as a purification process on my soul. I knew that something
special was taking place.

We didn't have time to discuss the whole teaching
because I had to catch a train in the early evening. I
soon realized they were saying that Sun Moon actually is
the Messiah. I asked them outright: "Is it true what
you are saying, that Sun Myung Moon is the Christ?"
When they said yes I had a tremendous experience. My
spirit was almost leaving my body with such a joyous
feeling. I then recalled that my father had once told

me he had a vision one night that Christ was really on earth and was an Oriental man. Of course, I didn't agree with him. I told him, "well, Daddy, that is wrong. When Jesus comes again he will come in the clouds. He will not be born all over again, like a human child."

I recalled too that when I was a high school student, I firmly believed that Jesus would come back to earth in my lifetime. I was taught in those days that the cosmic winter has ended and the cosmic spring had arrived. Having had some Rosicrucian background, that was very significant to me. I thought this had something to do with the new Age. My father used to teach me what he learned as a Rosicrucian, and it's related very closely to the Freemasons. So here I was listening to these Americans, convinced that God had led me to them and that I really should join their religious movement. At the same time I wanted to make sure that I wasn't letting Jesus down by accepting this new doctrine about Reverend Moon.

They promised to put me in contact with an American woman named Doris at the Unified Family center in London, and gave me the address before taking me to the railroad station in their car. They gave me a copy of Divine Principle, and I had taken a lot of quick notes on what they told me that afternoon. When I got back to England from Italy I spent about six weeks reading the book and studying my notes. I used to feel a threatening kind of sensation, like an evil force trying to stop me from reading them. It was like an evil presence trying to put fear into me so that I would stay away from these teachings. Although I felt some fear I decided after several weeks that I would go to the London center and hear some more about this religious teaching.

Then I could not find the slip of paper on which they had written the address. I thought I had put it into a safe and secure place, but I searched my room for almost a week and could not find it. I could just barely remember the name of the man in Rome and the church where I had met him, so I wrote to ask him for the London address. This was in 1967 when the Unified Family was hardly known in England and one could not easily locate them. I had the feeling there was some sort of spiritual battle going on. Satan didn't want me to make that contact, but I was sure God made the condition that nothing could stop me.

When I received the address from Rome I wrote to the girl who was the church's missionary all by herself in London. I didn't have her phone number and I didn't hear from her. I thought that was very strange. After waiting several weeks I finally prayed, "God, if you really want me to go and hear the <u>Divine</u> <u>Principle</u> in my lifetime then by next Monday you have to give me a sign." That weekend I spent in Paris, and when I got back on Monday the answer was there. She said the strangest thing had happened with my letter. She had put it inside a book, reshelved the book and forgotten about it. On Friday she had been dusting the bookshelf; this book fell out and there was my letter. Now I became more confident because I believed this was a revelation from God.

We had only a few opportunities to be together because the center was a considerable distance from my quarters; she had many duties, and I was busy with my work in the children's clinic. When I decided to spend Christmas with some relatives in Germany I asked her for the address of the Unification headquarters in Frankfurt. I stayed there for several days and was fortunate that Peter Koch was there to help me. He told me very much about Sun Myung Moon whom he knew personally and held in great reverence. He also gave me counsel about the importance of prayer and pointed out that we really must try to achieve perfection in this life. When I prayed in the name of Sun Myung Moon I experienced tremendous power over evil, which I had never experienced as a Christian. It must surely be a sign of salvation as well.

I determined then to join the church as soon as I returned to London, but another strange thing happened. I do not have a good sense of direction, and I got lost in the streets of London looking for the Church center. I simply stopped and prayed that God would give me some kind of sign to help me find my way. Suddenly I saw a woman standing outside one of the doors and I wondered whether that could be the center. As I watched she beckoned and I saw her go through the doorway, but I realized that the door had never opened and she had just passed through the locked door. Maybe she was an angel but she looked so natural that it didn't worry me.

In January I told my sister and her husband that I was about to join the Church and was moving in with the other members. There were only five of us there but we prayed very much, spent the evenings discussing the

<u>Divine</u> <u>Principle</u> and explaining it to anybody we could bring there to listen. I had hardly become accustomed to the life of this community when we got word from Young Oon Kim that a blessing was to take place that year in Europe. Although I now felt quite comfortable with the demands of celibacy, and although I did not consider myself a fully trained member, I was asked to give the names of three brothers with whom I might possibly be matched. I really did not feel ready to make such a suggestion, and the fact is that I was not matched that time because there wasn't anybody suitable for me.

Later that year I was sent to Jordan as a missionary, where I was able to do social work among the dependent children and witnessed to their parents. I had told the leaders in England that it made no difference who my husband was to be because I believed that Reverend Moon would make the right choice for me, especially since I knew that my future mate and I would share the same religion. I was convinced that sharing the same religious beliefs was the essence of a God-centered marriage. I knew from experience that no matter how different two persons are, the mutual love of God can overcome any differences and you can learn to love each other.

Even so, they wanted me to name one or two brothers whom I would see as a prospective spouse because there was another blessing coming up in 1970. Even though I felt it didn't matter to whom I was matched, I did mention one young man who was then in England while I was in Jordan. Then I got a kind of revelation that he was not for me, and I felt in my very heart that it

wasn't right and that it wouldn't take place. My premonition was correct. He did some irresponsible thing -
not a sin - and they disqualified him from the blessing
for the time being. Then I suggested another person's
name, who is actually my present husband, and I felt
good about that.

He was also an Englishman, although I would have
been ready to marry a brother from another race or
another country. Later on he told me that he had had a
dream or a vision that I was to be his wife but he never
revealed this to the church leaders. They sent me a
telegram saying that a mate had been chosen for me and
that I was to return to England and prepare for the
blessing. I felt comfortable with that because among
all the brothers I knew and respected he was one in whom
I could have great confidence. The general practice in
the Church is that Reverend Moon matches the prospective
spouses even though they may be persons who had never
seen each other. I would have been willing to accept
such a matching. In the actual case, my husband is a
deep spiritual person with whom I could express whatever
feelings I had. He was actually four years younger than
I, but I saw no reason for being embarrassed about that.

We were part of the so-called 777 blessing which
brought in members from all over the world to be married
in Seoul, Korea. That was in 1970, and we had seen each
other only occasionally before that. We left a full
planeload out of London and stopped briefly in Tokyo
before going on to Korea. One of the conditions to
qualify for marriage was that we each had to have three
spiritual children, that is, individuals who came into
the Church as a result of our witnessing. Actually I

had seven spiritual children, and he had two. When we came back to England he stayed with the brothers at the center, and I stayed with the sisters. In some instances the newly married couple is separated to do an indemnity for a fairly lengthy time, each going off on a different mission for the Church. Since I was considered "old" at the time of marriage - I was thirty-one - we were given permission to live together after the usual forty-day wait.

We remained in England for over five years doing the large variety of tasks that are common to the members of our Church. My husband did much more fundraising than I, and I did much more lecturing than he. One of our joint ventures was a lecture series on the Unification teaching on marriage and family. We experienced some practical difficulties in our personal relations. My training in psychology and social work was of great help in getting us over some troublesome times. It was clear to us - and we understood this from the beginning - that there is nothing automatic that makes a Moonie marriage more successful than other marriages.

We have two boys who were born three years apart, and they have been a great source of joy to us. We see God's beauty and goodness in our children, and my husband often says that they are a proof of God's approval of our own matching and blessing. The children are so very special that we can see why God really wanted to bring us together in the first place. Since we returned to South Africa we have not been living in a Unified Family community. When we first arrived there some friends of my mother provided a cottage for us to live. It is in a small village near Johannesburg where my husband is employed with a law firm while I continue to do the work of the Church.

Because of the racial barriers it is more difficult to do witnessing than it is in most other countries. We have less than a dozen white church members in that area but well over fifty colored members. Since Reverend Moon introduced the concept of home church in 1978 and encouraged us all over the world to put it into practice, I have been able to do this among the whites in our neighborhood. My husband keeps very busy, is faithful to the teachings of the Church, but has found it difficult to adjust to the hot climate of South Africa. We are now planning to return to England where we may be able to cooperate fully in the work of the Church, and where our sons may get a proper British education.

IV

DAVID — JESUIT PRODUCT

When I joined the Unified Family there were less than fifteen members in all of Britain, and most of them lived in a big house in a very nice suburb of South London. It was like a small religious community, the leaders of which were a married couple, Dennis and Doris Orme. In a sense she was the one who brought the Church from America where she had been converted by Reverend Moon's first missionary to the United States, Young Oon Kim. I suppose that could be called a clear lineage on a straight line right back to the apostolic founder in Korea.

Hardly anybody knew anything about this new religious group. Certainly I didn't. I was in college at Cambridge in the Autumn of 1969, when a friend of mine told me he'd about given up his job in a bank to go live in an Israeli kibbutz, but instead he joined this religious community. He didn't tell me a lot about it. He said it was started off by somebody from Korea and would I care to come visit them over my Christmas holidays. So I did. I went along really out of curiosity to see what Robert was into, because he was a person of integrity and I respected him. While I was there he said maybe I'd like to hear some lectures about their beliefs. There were no workshops or seminars in those days. So, gradually, over my Christmas vacation I heard all of the _Divine_ _Principle_.

For the next six weeks I had no contact with their house, and stayed in Cambridge where I studied and read a mimeo copy of the Divine Principle. It challenged me personally and forced me to rethink my whole philosophy of living. In the end I came to the decision that in its main essentials the Principle was true. While I was at the University, I had stopped going to church even though I had been raised a Roman Catholic and had attended a Jesuit school. I stopped believing a lot of things I had learned earlier. In a sense I was an agnostic, not an atheist, because I kept an open mind and thought there might be a God. I felt that I didn't really know God, so what's the point of me saying that I believe there is a God, or I believe there isn't, if I don't know.

I think the Jesuits had taught me very well all the arguments in support of religious beliefs. Other people at the University who had a very good Catholic training said the same thing. They knew all the apologetics, but they didn't seem to have any spiritual experience. So we came to a point where we started thinking: "Why do we believe these things? What difference do they really make in my life?" I used to read Lives of the Saints and tell myself "these people have something that I don't have, and I want to find out what that is." So, gradually I started looking at my intellectual beliefs, and I asked myself: "How different would my life be if I did not believe these things" and I had to admit honestly that my beliefs didn't make much difference in my life. So, bit by bit I'd been throwing things out until I came to the basic position of saying "there may be a God, but I don't know."

That wasn't a satisfying state of mind for me. I wasn't content to leave it there. I wanted to find out. What I was looking for, I think, was a direct contact, or a personal experience of God. First of all, I got interested in Zen Buddhism because it seemed to emphasize experience and deemphasize theology. In that sort of way I had a number of experiences that came through nature, of seeing particularly striking, dramatic and beautiful scenery which moved me very much and gave me a sense that what I was seeing was more than just the surface phenomenon. I had the impression that there was some vague presence beyond what I actually saw and that this presence was trying to reach me and touch me.

In spite of this kind of psychic experience I was getting quite depressed and confused. Even though I thought that there is something permanent beyond the changing world and its shifting circumstances, I did not conclude that it was God, either personal or impersonal. I started praying in my own sort of way, which was a cry from the heart: "What's going on? Is there anybody out there? Please give me some answers." I felt that if I could somehow reach this thing then it would answer my questions about what's the true value of life. What gives it sense and purpose? What happened when I met the Church and started to hear the Principle was that somehow the loose ends were tied up and I could understand my experience of nature then as an experience of God. That something that had been at a distance suddenly came much closer. I started to have some sense of the presence of God, particularly as I began to pray.

It may seem strange for a person of my Catholic upbringing to say that I learned to pray only after I became a member of the Unification family. Of course, I knew the typical prayers that are said in the Mass and the Rosary,and for confession and communion. I certainly understood the meaning of the words we were reciting, but they never seemed to have a real connection with anyone outside of me, like the saints or Jesus or God. Now it was different as a Unificationist. We have simple morning service when all members of the center come together. In content it is a bit similar to the pledge we make every morning, and we usually sing some holy songs. Then we have prayer, which is spontaneous and very personal in the sense that it's not a formula. Then we pray together as a group. We have a unison prayer. Some pray very quietly, but one or another may be moved to a vocal expression of praise and glory to God.

I had expected that my parents might be distressed about my joining another church. Initially they had several practical objections, mainly to do with living in a community where you give up all your personal belongings. What happens in a few years if you change your mind? There is no economic security either now or in the future. They didn't have religious objections when I joined because they didn't know much about the teaching. Shortly afterward they read the Divine Principle, and that set them back a bit because they profoundly disagreed with it. I still find it difficult to talk with them about the teachings. They like the church members they've met. They enjoyed the social and cultural functions they've attended. They think maybe there is some truth here, and they finally said, "well you're old enough to make up your own mind."

My brother and three sisters are also Catholics like my parents, and we had a couple of arguments at the very beginning. I think I wasn't very tactful with them. I was sort of young and over-enthusiastic, but I learned. They have seen all the negative publicity heaped on Reverend Moon and the Church, but they certainly did not become negative about us. They've never begged me to leave the Church and have never made the kind of public attacks that have been publicized from the families of some members. They are sure that the jury findings in The Daily Mail legal cases were in error, and I think they have a kind of secret admiration for the part I played in that judicial procedure.

In the beginning they were not sure whether I had become a seminarian in this new religious community. They knew I went out with women just like the other University students, and even that I had contemplated marriage with a girl they knew. I certainly had not planned a life of celibacy even though chastity and celibacy became central virtues for me in the Unified Family. It wasn't until May 1978 that I got the call from Reverend Moon to come to a matching. This was a very emotional and very spiritual experience. After matching all the others in the room Reverend Moon spoke directly and quietly to me. He gave a quick five-minute assessment of my character, and revealed things that only my close friends could know about me, and even one item I had never told anybody. I was really impressed that he knew my deepest aspirations and deepest longings. Then he asked the rhetorical question: "What sort of wife do you think would be good for you?" And all I could stammer out was, "probably not British."

Before he selected my future spouse, he gave a character description of a person who would be a good wife for me. No girl I had known in earlier years fit that description, but I liked what he said and thought this would be the ideal wife for me. We were the last couple to be matched that day, and when he brought us together I asked her whether she wanted to go outside and talk about it. I said it wasn't necessary, and she agreed "It's O.K. by me." I felt great confidence that this was the person for me. Afterwards, another Korean, a long-time friend of hers, said "that was an amazing description Reverend Moon foretold about the woman who would be a good wife for you. The description he gave fits exactly her nature and her character." What happened there assured me that God was choosing the person with whom I could build an eternal relationship. It is interesting that I had only seen her once or twice before, but had never spoken to her.

This was the Church's first public group wedding in Britain. There had previously been only one couple married among our Church members. In this instance the mass wedding ceremony of 118 couples took place on the day after the matching and the Holy Wine ceremony. On Saturday we had the matching, and on Sunday evening we were at the wedding reception. I tried to ring my parents up and invite them to the reception, but they were out of the country. So they didn't find out until after the event. My wife had to leave immediately because she was teaching at a university in Germany. When she came back to London in August we took out the marriage license and had a civil marriage. We then had a small wedding reception, which my parents and family and some friends attended. The universal custom in the Unified Family is that the couple postpones the actual consummation of the marriage, but the period of separation varies vastly. Reverend Moon sets a minimum period of forty days. With some couples, especially younger members, it's often several years. What happens now is that the matching is not followed by the wedding for about three years. In our case we had to wait only four months.

For the most part this long delay between the matching and the wedding, and between the wedding and consummation, is a healthy opportunity to prepare prayerfully for the serious vocation of married life. Even if you are working in different countries you can write about what you are doing and get to learn about each other. In a practical sense I think it enhances the importance of chastity before marriage. This may be seen as a heavy sacrifice by some, or an indemnity, but you have been living a celibate life all along. On the other hand, we don't think there is something heroic about abstaining from sex, even though our modern culture seems to be almost obsessed by sex. Not all of the couples who are matched persevere finally to go through with the wedding, and that too may be a sign that even in our system it's good to take your time about getting married.

One of the interesting developments in membership over the years is the growing numbers of people who are attached to the Church and do not enter full-time into our work and our community life. We have been calling them associate members, in some sense like lay parishioners in the Roman church. They come for lectures and discussions about the <u>Divine</u> <u>Principle</u> and are converted to the beliefs of the Church. Instead of coming into the center, they keep their jobs and homes and families when they become Unification Church members. I see the way ahead of the Church as being through that sort of association. The Church will move out into the community more. Also, there are the core members, a lot of couples in Britain and in the whole of Europe, who are blessed, married, and have now come together to start their family.

I think Reverend Moon's idea for families is that the blessed couples should go out and live in the community where their family should be an example to all others. I think we'll see, in some respects, a decentralization of the Unified Family. As members begin to have their own children and have to bring them up, they will be more permanently involved in the larger community. These couples are not living in a center or working for the Church, but they are contributing tithes. After all, the business enterprises of the Church, while they are many, cannot begin to employ all the members. This fact is sometimes forgotten by our enemies who see the church as a vast monolithic economic enterprise engaging the total life and activity of every member.

All of this is wrapped up in my own spiritual conversion. Coming to an understanding of the nature of God, accepting the teachings of the <u>Divine</u> <u>Principle</u>, and learning how to communicate with God through prayer, all of this is the beginning of religious conversion.

Reverend Moon has always urged that the love of God is the service of our fellowmen. This basic concept was with the Church from the beginning in Korea, and it has been systematically applied in what we call the home church movement. It was worked out on a large scale in Britain by the unmarried seminarians who were instructed to give personal service to a circle of 360 households. That's a symbolic number of homes that became their parish, or in biblical terms, their Canaan. This is not witnessing in the direct mode. We are there to serve, not to evangelize, although the inevitable question is bound to arise: Why are you doing this? What's in it for you? They want to know if you get paid, especially if you are back to help someone who has rejected you. When they ask why you do it you may tell them about your faith. Many are really interested to know because they are intrigued with this unexpected offer of service.

The service to them is not conditional, and you tell people about your faith only when they ask. My understanding of everything Reverend Moon has been saying about home church - and he's talked an awful lot about it in the last few years - is that you don't give them a pamphlet or a brochure or a homily. You don't say "I'm coming to bring you the truth." The primary purpose is to find ways just to serve their needs. Whether they are nice to you, or nasty, you keep trying to be of help to them. This ties in closely with our whole theological teaching on restoration. It is Abel's mission and purpose to serve Cain. You don't just love those who listen to your religious teaching. You love people, whether they listen or not, whether they are nice to you or not, whether they thank you or not.

Of course, it's difficult to do that. If someone
is unpleasant to you your instinctive reaction may be,
"I'll never speak to them again." But if you can
control that reaction and go back again and do something
for them you feel really good inside. You feel not only
that you've overcome a challenge, or that you are
getting somewhere in your spiritual development, but
especially that you are serving the will of God. You
often find old people who need help doing their
shopping, tending their garden, cleaning the house.
Sometimes families, especially young mothers, want their
kids looked after. Sometimes with people who are old or
who have problems, you're just listening. A lot of
people are lonely in a big city and are happy just to
have someone to talk to. The individual Moonies are
fulfilling their religious vocation in this way.

Other aspects of the faith and its practice go
beyond service to God and to other human beings. The
problem of religious persecution seems to have occurred
against all organized religion at one time or another.
The Unification Church has had more than its share of
animosity in the Third World as well as in Western
society, even here in Britain. Our mission of witnessing and of service has been slowed down by widespread
negativity. We thought we could offset the prejudiced
news media in Britain by bringing a libel suit against
The Daily Mail, which published a two-page spread with
the headline that our Church "breaks up families."
There were the usual charges, made in other countries as
well as here, that youngsters were being lured into
"this sinister sect," that deception and brainwashing
were Moonie methods for gaining and retaining members in
the Church. We were sure that with competent lawyers we

could easily disprove these allegations, or that the newspaper would find it impossible to prove such charges.

We were wrong, and mainly I think because we underestimated our enemies. A Christian group, the Deo Gloria Trust, are in strong animosity to all religious movements, Children of God, Hare Krishna, Scientology, Transcendental meditation. They are biblical fundamentalists who brought sociological and psychological arguments against us. They said we are breaking up families when we accept a new member in the Church. Their hidden reason for attacking us was that we were doing the work of the Devil. They don't say that because such statements would not cut much ice in contemporary society. Another group, called FAIR (Family Action Information and Rescue) has a range of people. It used to be people of a left-wing tint, but more recently it has gathered in Anglicans and evangelical ministers, plus parents of Church members. Some of them stay involved with the group even if their daughter or son leaves the Unification Church. This group has had support from Americans like Daphne Green and John Clark. There was even one case in which the family flew in Joel Alexander from the States to deprogram their son.

Unfortunately, The Daily Mail made the case of a five-month trial into a propaganda attack against the Church. The jury accepted the negative statements of hostile witnesses. The Church was ordered to pay enormous court costs, and the court also recommended that the Church's tax-free status "should be investigated by the Inland Revenue Department, on the ground that it is a political organization." The Attorney General has appealed to the Charity Commissioners to have our tax-exempt status removed. Our argument is that there was no evidence in the case to show that we are a political organization. People talked about the Church's connection with the government of Korea, about our stance on anti-communism everywhere, about Reverend Moon's support of President Nixon in the Watergate investigations. Our argument is that, in any case, you can't remove the charity status of any British charities because of something that was done in America by people who happen to share the same religious beliefs.

As a consequence of such notoriety and such bigotry the basic mission of the Unified Family has been hindered. Witnessing has become more difficult; fewer people are willing to come to the center for discussions and lectures. Dialogue on any level is very difficult once someone is really filled with fear, and I don't say that just on speculation. I have talked to parents who had contact with our enemies but who then plucked up courage to visit us to get the facts. They said that they were told things about us that really scared them. They had received propaganda and warnings from the American "anti-cult" groups. Many of them came to us in search of the truth and ultimately became our friends.

V

MARGARET — MISSIONER TO MANAGUA

Ever since I was a little girl I had a strong belief in the providence of God. Although I am a convert from the Catholic Church to the Unification Church I did not have a spiritual conversion like persons who are non-believers and then come to know God. I always knew that God answers prayers. My mother used to tell me and my brothers and sisters that we should pray and ask God what he wants us to do with our lives. You would ask if you should become a nun, or get married. My father died when I was sixteen; he was a very pious man, and he thought it would be good for me to enter the convent.

So we had religion and God in our family life. All the children went to the public Mittelschule in Karlsruhe, where we regularly got religious instructions. The priest would come to the school and prepare us for our first confession, for receiving communion and for the sacrament of confirmation. I went to Mass every Sunday, but I didn't always understand the sermons because the priest seemed to be talking heavy theology. When I had problems about religion I would ask my mother. I was not clear whether I should pray to Jesus rather than to God and whether Jesus also was God. I wanted my life to be something special, but I never knew how to direct my heart. I was looking for a higher purpose, I guess. I wasn't looking for a way to get out of the Church. As far as I was concerned there just wasn't any other church.

When I finished the customary nine years of schooling - that is, for young people who were not going to enter the University - I was accepted in an apprenticeship training for three years in the grocery business. What this meant is that I became a secretary, doing clerical work for the manager. This was interesting enough; I learned a lot and made many friends, but I wasn't satisfied with it as a life commitment. I took evening courses in language and psychology at the popular university, more to be with my friends than to get much learning. One of the courses I enjoyed most was in Yoga, which was being taken also by a young man I liked very much.

Actually we became very good friends, but we did not think in terms of a serious lasting relationship. We were both interested in God and religion and the Bible, and had long discussions about the Church. He is the one who told me about a youth group that was meeting at the university, who turned out to be members of the Unification Church. I was not impressed with his description, but he said "why don't you go over there and take a look at it yourself?" So one night when I was free I went there. When I looked for them at the school they weren't there, but I got directions to their address. It was a little apartment with several rooms, and there were just two church members there, a German girl and one girl from Finland who couldn't speak German.

They told me about a special book they called the Divine Principle which seemed to be a combination of the Old and the New Testaments. Either they weren't explaining it very well or I wasn't understanding it very well. Some of it was a little bit strange, but I thought it was interesting enough to come back for more. It was also that once I start to investigate something I want really to go through it and finish it. Therefore, I visited them frequently. In the beginning I didn't agree with everything they said, especially about the failure of Jesus and about the second advent of the Messiah. Sometimes I thought I should interrupt them and teach them the truth I had learned in the catechism and in bible history. But the principle of creation seemed so clear as a new way for precise explanation. I felt that if some part of it is true, and another part I cannot understand, I must dig into it and really study till I know it.

Perhaps I am a slow learner; and maybe I am very cautious. I actually took more than a year to study and question and discuss these teachings. I was reading the Bible and making comparisons with the Divine Principle. I had to be very careful because I thought of Christ's words about the wolf in sheep's clothing. It was a time of real struggle, and on some days I believed and on other days I did not. I really wanted to know from God the Father what is the truth. I knew that if this is really true I would have to follow it entirely. I asked my older sister, but she could not help. I thought about the Sister catechist I had in school, but I didn't know where she now lived. I was not close enough to the parish priest to ask him.

All the doubts disappeared one day like a direct answer to my prayers. It was a deep emotional experience, where God showed me very clearly in my heart that these teachings were true. I understood that God was calling me to a new life, to give up my family and to go in a strange and different direction. It almost broke my heart to tell this to my mother. She is so deeply committed to the Catholic Church that she repeated "how can you give up the true church to go to another religion?" On my part I was fully convinced and I felt in my heart that God was calling me. I begged her to pray to God in her own way to see if this was His will. I said "This is a sacrifice for myself and I know it is very hard on you. I don't want to leave you alone but only because God called me could I do that." She understood in the end that I was not just talking, and not just running away from her, but that I was deeply serious.

Since I had steady employment I had to give notice that I would leave the job at the end of the year, 1973, so that they could find a person to replace me. I left Karlsruhe and went to our training center just outside of Frankfurt, where I spent two months becoming accustomed to the life of the Church members, listening to lectures on the <u>Divine</u> <u>Principle</u> and on the life and mission of Reverend Moon. I studied and prayed more than ever in my life before. Paul Werner and his wife Crystal were the leaders of the Church in Germany, but they were also spending a lot of time doing missionary work in America.

My first assignment as a member of the Church was at our center in Regensberg, where we had two people whose income from their jobs supported the rest of us. We had a team there of eight people who spent their time witnessing to all the young people we could reach. By this time I knew enough about the <u>Divine</u> <u>Principle</u> that I could explain it pretty clearly to others, and I soon learned the techniques and method of approaching complete strangers on the street and engaging them in religious discussion. It wasn't always easy, but I did have some success in attracting people. This team moved around Germany, two months in this city and two months there. From Regensberg we went to Bremen, then to Frankfurt for a time, then to Essen and back to Regensberg.

In the beginning of 1975 we learned that missionaries were to be sent out to all countries in the world, and we were invited to volunteer to go to a foreign land. Each country was to get three missionaries, an international team of one from Germany, one from Japan and one from America. Paul Werner gathered the volunteers in Frankfurt and outlined the plans for mission work. He had a pile of travel folders from the different countries, and he could say something about them because he had travelled extensively. We were asked if we had a preference, and I volunteered for Nicaragua.

Thirteen of us who had volunteered for Central America gathered for a spiritual workshop in Nassau, the Bahamas, where we also had some quick lessons in the Spanish language. I was a little nervous because I didn't speak much English and knew even less Spanish;

and I was going into a strange country. I didn't even know where Nicaragua was located. There were no Moonies in that country, and I was the first one to go there in April, 1975. Of course, I was sustained by prayer and by the conviction that God was calling me there to do his work.

For the first time also I was briefly in America when I flew to Miami to change planes for Nicaragua. The Lord does provide for those who have faith in Him. That morning in the waiting room of the airport a girl smiled at me, and we went together on the plane. She started to talk to me in English when she saw that I was by myself. We managed to communicate, and she said she wondered about me because I was alone and couldn't speak Spanish. She was surprised when I said I didn't have anyone to meet me at Managua, nor any definite address to go to. She said "Maybe I will ask my parents if you can stay at our house till you get settled." When we got to the airport her parents were there to pick her up, and they agreed to take me to their home. What was also good was that her father spoke some German. I was very thankful because I believed that God had worked this out for me. I couldn't have done it by myself.

These were very kind and generous Catholic people, and after three days they helped me find a German family with whom I could stay. None of them asked me about my religion because they probably thought I was a Catholic. I had been warned not to volunteer any information and to be very careful in the beginning. The first thing I had to do was to find employment to support myself and to pay rent for an apartment in the city. Soon the American missionary sister came; then after two months the Japanese brother came so that we could start our mission together. We all had to have at least a part-time jobs because that is required to hold the visa.

We were there just before the Sandinista revolution began. It was a good time to do the home church program. To help people in their homes, talk with them, go there to serve them, began as a good project. Missionaries had been trained in home church even before the summer when Reverend Moon took the seminarians to England. There are always poor families and elderly people who need help, and we made many good friends that way even though we were only learning how to speak the language. As soon as the revolution started we couldn't work any more in this way. We still kept contact with certain families who have confidence in us. You could no longer just walk up and knock on somebody's door because they feared we could be from the security police.

Of course, when the revolution got under way there was shooting going on all over the place. You had to be aware that anything could happen. We always tried to be home before dark, and we had to be careful of the families we went to visit because the government at that time was looking for young people who were involved in politics. Some mothers would send their children to our house to be protected. So, when people came to us we gave them short talks about the Divine Principle. Sometimes our brothers went out to teach people in their homes and were stopped by the police. One policeman with a gun grabbed the brother's handbag and threw it to the ground because he thought it had some explosives. When he opened it and found there were only books and pamphlets, he asked, "Are you a Christian?" Then he apologized very courteously.

After the successful revolution to remove Somoza in 1979 there was a period when we made many good contacts. We were able to help the poor people get food and some schooling for their children. Religion was important to them and was encouraged by the new government, but we had to remember that we were foreigners and our Unified Family was regarded like the North American Protestants. They had already kicked out the Mormons and the Jehovah's Witnesses. We have to be quiet also about our political beliefs, because the stand of our Church is rather strongly anti-Marxist. It would harm us rather than do any good if we spoke out in politics.

In the Church center in Managua we had three young ladies who lived with us as full-time members. We also had a growing number of people who are in sympathy with us. Sometimes you expect much more result for the large effort you put in because you really want to bring good results. At other times I feel that I cannot go there as the first missionary to the country and expect already to have a large harvest. This is historic. I feel we must put in tears and sweat and effort, and also keep praying that God receives this offering and gives His blessing when the time comes. All our members everywhere have this dream because they have great faith in the message of Reverend Moon. One of our members said the heavenly Father told her that we have to wait; the time is not yet here. I have hope also. I never was actually discouraged.

We felt it was wise not to incorporate legally as a church in Nicaragua. The Protestants are organized in a kind of movement, but they are considered North American foreigners in a predominantly Roman Catholic population. We didn't advertise ourselves as a church, and we didn't work so much as a movement, but rather just person to person. So, we didn't face any real opposition. In other words, while the country officially proclaims freedom of religion, and no one is persecuted for religious reasons, we prefer not to work openly as missionaries.

Life in the Unified Family is very disciplined and ascetic, and we expect it to be even more so when we are on the foreign missions. But I never had the feeling of being restricted. There were many difficult times, and I am grateful that in all these experiences I learned so much and my life was enriched. I felt that God was always at my side, and I was not really isolated from my brothers and sisters in the Family. We have a special World Mission Department in New York that takes care of the foreign missionaries. We have round-robin letters, and a church leader will visit us twice a year, and we also have regional meetings in Mexico of all the missionaries from the neighboring Central American countries. Every year something is going on, or somebody is coming through.

I almost feel that I am the mother of the Church in Nicaragua, not only because I was the first but also because I stay there while others come and go. The first American sister stayed for three years and then joined her husband who was in Egypt at the time. The Japanese brother was a reporter for a newspaper in

Tokyo. The government seemed to be suspicious of him. His wife came to be with him in 1980, and they both made many friends, but it seemed better to us that they leave the country in the following year. So I was alone again, except for the three converts we made, and I prayed very intensely for the people living there. Much is being done for the poor people; they eat better now, and their children are learning to read. But there is great unrest, and I really could see how God is suffering when there are so many people who ignore Him.

One of the happy events of my life was in December, 1978, when Reverend Moon invited many missionaries to come to New York for a matching. This had been one of my prayers to God, because marriage and family are so important in our movement. I knew that time would come when I would be faced with this event. I decided to pray every day for five minutes just to be ready to receive God's call and to receive the person he was preparing for me. I think Reverend Moon respects missionaries in a special way, and we were the first ones who were called up to be matched.

It was in the Grand Ballroom of the World Mission Center in New York where there were more than a thousand members in line, sisters on one side and brothers on the other side. I prayed sincerely, "Please, God, Heavenly Father, may Your will be done." Reverend Moon looked at each of us, and I had this feeling he could really grasp our whole personality. He asked for our age sometimes. He didn't ask so much about our education. I think he rather looked at our heart situation and at our level of understanding and growth. So he suggested Mike, an American brother, for me, and when I saw him for the first time I thought that he looks like a good father for my children. Then we went to another room to talk it over. Some people take hours to decide whether they want to accept Reverend Moon's matching. We had the feeling right away that our Heavenly Father was pleased with this choice at that moment.

When the Holy Wine ceremony took place we both knew that this was a permanent bond between us, made with the approval of God and His messenger. I, of course, had prepared myself in prayer. I thought the choice a very good one and was prepared to accept it completely on the foundation of faith. He had been in the Church for seven years, had looked forward to the vocation of marriage and said practically the same thing. After the ceremony I went back to Nicaragua, and my husband continued his work in the States. We kept in touch mainly with letters, and sometimes by phone, and that way we learned a great deal about each other. This is something like an engagement period, but for us we knew that we were already in the same lineage. Then we went again to New York for the mass wedding at Madison Square Garden in July, 1982.

Even after that we did not begin to live together. We visited with his parents who live in Berkeley, California and who received me with great fondness. They had a party for us and gathered the other relatives and friends. They are good people. More recently we went to Karlsruhe in Germany to visit with my mother. It was the first time I had seen her since I left to join the Unified Family. Over the years we had exchanged letters monthly, and once in a while one of my sisters would write to me. My mother liked Mike after the strangeness wore off, and I think she has been very brave and loving in her acceptance of us as a couple. She still prays that I come back to the Catholic Church, but also wants me to do God's will.

What we look forward to now is to have our own blessed children. My age is already over thirty, and I don't think we can have a very large family. We must look out for our health and our capacity to grow. This is especially true because we want really good children, not necessarily a lot of them. Meanwhile, we both carry on the tasks that the Church has assigned to us.

VI

LIONEL — TO BE A SCHOLAR

There wasn't much religion in my family, or among the young people I hung around with, or in the schools I attended. My parents are of the Jewish background and went to the synagogue twice a year; and I went less often than that. I guess it was early on that I came to a half-formed notion that God wasn't in tune with the world - if he existed at all. I had relatively few Christian contacts, and had no real interest in Judaism for many years. I went to a private prep school in New England, where we had to take a course in the Bible. For a while, in high school, I was interested in Yoga and meditation, and for about a year I was on a macrobiotic diet. As a student at Harvard I was deep into science, took a major in biochemistry, planned on going to Harvard Medical School and then becoming a research scientist.

My years as an undergraduate at Harvard were a period of great radical activity. In the spring of my freshman year they occupied University Hall and called the student strike. When I was a sophomore they marched through the streets of Harvard Square, where rioting was met with tear gas, and I was in the midst of that. I had friends who were political radicals, but I watched how quickly the radical groups broke into factions and fought among themselves. So I became more interested in a sort of cultural radicalism of the environmental movement. I spent a summer on a environmental project protesting nuclear power in Vermont. I became interested in alternative ways of living, and as I began to move in that direction my interest in science gradually declined.

As a matter of fact, I went through a disillusionment with what I had thought was my calling to be a scientist. I had grown up with that idea which came mainly from my parents, but also from my own choice because over the years in school I did very well in my courses in science. I had thought I would become a great research scientist and help solve the problems of the world through science. Even while I was still in college I began to feel that science was not the answer to the world's problems; that no matter how many scientific studies were made, the life condition of most people was not going to improve unless some more basic changes were made, particularly in the way people treated one another.

After college graduation I spent about six months on the road hitchhiking across the country, and became a real hippie with a beard and long hair and beads. It was really like an adventure, breaking away from the academic world where I had been living so long. I lived with all kinds of people: hoboes and drifters, sheep herders and poor people in the barrios of New Mexico where they fought over heroin every night. I wanted to experience where people are really at in this world. So, that was an act of searching on my part. To me it was a kind of liberation and a chance to discover something new and different for myself in my life.

On the way west I went from one commune to another, and other young people were also coming and going. If you wanted to join one of those communities maybe there was some leader who would be holding the group together, but if that leader left the thing would break up. If a fellow and a girl met there they might pair off and split from the group. These people didn't have any systematic way of forming themselves into a lasting community. Even though they talked a lot about love it seemed to be pretty selfish, and the communes were very unstable. Some of them were into Eastern religions, a sort of quasi-Hinduism or Buddhism, but with individualistic types of religious practices. Sometimes they chanted mantras in separate and private meditation. I couldn't take Christianity seriously at all because the fundamentalists I met didn't seem to have anything intelligent to offer. They were individualists too, and I did not find any encouragement for social identity or community.

I didn't believe in God at the time, but I came to feel that there must be some higher force beyond myself that was vaguely giving me some guidance. This feeling stayed with me when I arrived in Berkeley. I also had a premonition that this is the place where I would meet a group with whom I could make friends and perhaps be able to stay for a while. I felt so strongly about it that I actually gave away my backpack and sleeping bag to a young fellow who was headed north. I spent one night with a crazy messianic family that had a restaurant on Telegraph Avenue and a Messiah named Allen Noonan. He believed he had revelations from the planet Venus. At four o'clock in the morning there was a loud ruckus outside my room. Somebody wanted to vacuum the hallway;

the other fellow wanted to sleep. I thought these guys just can't get together. So I left that crazy house and looked around. Then I met the Moonies and went to their house.

There was a woman over near the campus selling sandwiches, and she wanted to talk about religion and the better life for human beings. I didn't buy the sandwich but I did accept the invitation to her house for dinner, and had a very nice time. She and her friends told me about a Korean, Mr. Sang Choi, who was giving great lectures in San Francisco; so I went across the Bay to hear him. He was very animated when he spoke; and really put himself into what he was saying. I was more impressed by his manner than anything else because I didn't understand half of what he was saying. They told me that the Oakland center was part of Mr. Choi's San Francisco family.

This was in 1972, just about the same time that Dr. Mose Durst, who later became the American President of the Unification Church, joined the movement. I decided to go to a weekend workshop at the Oakland residence, and I liked what I heard there. I realized at that workshop that these people really did have a spirituality which emphasized self-sacrifice for the sake of the unity of the larger group. This was different from other communes I had visited, where each person was out for himself, or herself, where they were all doing their own thing. Up to then I was pretty critical of the groups I had encountered on the road, but these people had a real concern for others.

My second night at the workshop, I had a very vivid dream. I was hitchhiking along a wooded lane in some suburb, and this bright yellow car, like a Rolls Royce, stopped and there were two women in the car. One of them looked a little bit like my mother. She was the workshop leader. The other one was Onni, who at the end of 1973 was married to Mose Durst. I didn't meet her until the next day, when I recognized her as the woman in the dream. So I got in the car. I hardly ever remember my dreams, but then I had another dream. At that time I was still wearing hippie long hair and a beard. But in this dream I was a little boy with short hair, sitting on an Oriental carpet and playing with rulers. You can understand the symbolism: rulers and principles; oriental and rebirth. It's all there. It didn't take me long to understand what these dreams meant.

In those days you couldn't just move in to the Oakland center on Dana Street. After the workshop you had to leave at night and then return the next morning on your own if you were interested. So, when I came back the next morning some of the people were cleaning out the garage, and I started to help them work. Onni came out and asked me if I wanted to join the group. She said "you can join up, but you have to live by our rules. The main rule is that we live like brothers and sisters, and we have no sexual relations for three years." I accepted that, and I think it was at that point that I felt I ought to join them. Two days later I shaved off my beard and cut my hair short. That was symbolic, but it was the real moment when I felt at home with the group. People didn't recognize me. I looked so different.

From then on I got into a regular program of prayer and work. Praying was something unfamiliar to me, either as an individual or with the group, but I was learning. Part of the process was a growing conviction that there exists a loving God who cares deeply about us human beings. First it was very difficult for me to pray, but I've grown to appreciate prayer. Someone said that "you should want to pray as much as you want to eat." I can't say that I enjoy it as much as I do eating. My prayer life has been mostly individual prayer, but I find that group prayer is easier than individual prayer. There is more support when you are in an environment where other people around you are praying.

The lectures I heard, the discussions we got into, even the routine of praying, all revolved around the teachings of <u>Divine</u> <u>Principle</u>. If there was a specific point in life when my spiritual conversion took place, I suppose that was the beginning of it, but I still had a lot to learn. Mostly I learned to pray during those first years in the Church when I lived in the center and we prayed in groups. When people pray individually you can hear how someone else in your group prays, particularly a leader; then you want to emulate how that person prays. There are also some specific instructions about making up prayer lists when we pray for specific people and specific things. I learned to do that. When you're praying in unison you have to develop an intensity so you won't get distracted by all the others around you. While I was in the center I prayed a lot in a group. Only in times of crisis, or on spiritual retreats, would I pray individually, but otherwise my personal prayer life was never that great.

To get back to Oakland; there was also a lot of work to do. The Family had a maintenance company with a wide variety of employment. I worked the graveyard shift, from midnight to eight in the morning, straightening up a restaurant, vacuuming in office buildings, cleaning carpets and rugs. I drove a truck for a while and did all kinds of jobs for about five months. I did fundraising on the streets of Oakland and San Francisco. then in October I moved from the Oakland Family to the New York Family.

The church work I did in New York for the next two years was a combination of fundraising and witnessing. I was also appointed center leader in Queens and Brooklyn, where I lectured regularly on the basic teachings of Divine Principle. Giving witness on the streets was a test of spiritual faith and physical endurance. I picked on only young people, and if I found one person a day who was interested that was very good actually. I had a little formula like, "Hullo, do you believe in God?" or I'd ask them "are you interested in a new philosophy, or a new religion?" It was kind of random. It meant just walking around the streets, looking for likely people, talking with them and inviting them to come hear a lecture.

It was there in New York, two and a half years after I had joined the church, I was abducted. It came as a complete surprise because I had no idea that my parents were so disaffected that they would try something like that. They had visited me several times and knew what I was doing, and seemed to like the fact that I didn't dress like a hippie any more. In fact, I had seen them three times in the spring of 1975, so I was completely unprepared. They had been in contact with one of those negative parents' groups led by Rabbi Maurice Davis, and I guess he got them all excited and put them in touch with Ted Patrick.

They took me up to Connecticut, locked me in a basement there and subjected me to brainwashing for almost six days. I was never left alone for more than an hour or two to snatch a nap. They rotated night and day, throwing water on my face to keep me awake and giving me constant verbal abuse. They had a big guard there named Goose, six foot five, so there was no way to escape. They kept working on me, and I finally just pretended to break down and go along with them. All of a sudden Ted Patrick became real nice and friendly, saying that he really cared about me and that my parents loved me very much. He showed me all the family photographs. That wasn't the end of it. They took me up to Canada for rehabilitation, which meant living in the house of a deprogrammer until they decided that I was stable enough and wouldn't go back to the Church.

My abductors said it would take about a month to rehabilitate me, but it gradually became clear to me that it was to be an indefinite period of time. They wanted me to sign a statement that the Church had brainwashed me. As a condition for releasing me they said I must do newspaper interviews and appear on television to explain what was wrong with the movement and how evil I knew the Reverend Moon to be. I realized that it was going to be hard to get away from them, but in the end I did arrange to escape.

Back in New York it wasn't easy to face my family again, but I was finally able to reconcile things pretty well. They begrudgingly accepted the fact that they were not able to change me. I was then twenty-four years old, and I guess it was part of my growing up process that I had never before confronted my parents with wanting to do something that was against their will. When I was in college I was fulfilling their expectation of me, that is, preparing to become a doctor or a scientist. Even while I was roaming the country as a hippie, they figured that was just a passing phase. But then, by joining the Unification Church I was really challenging, for the first time, the life program they had in mind for me. It took this kidnapping event to secure my independence from them.

About this time we got involved in activities that were more political than religious. Reverend Moon saw the bicentennial celebration as an opportunity to stress the providential destiny of America. Before Watergate he had been a frequent visitor to Capitol Hill, and he gave public support to Richard Nixon even in the midst of the Watergate hearings. The Madison Square rally in 1974, with the theme "God Bless America," was devoutly patriotic and religious. In the bicentennial year itself, 1976, the collective efforts of hundreds of Moonies went into two public extravaganzas, one in June at the Yankee Stadium, the other in September, at the Washington Monument. To be pro-American meant to be anti-Communist. Reverend Moon is convinced that America has a special role in the Providence of God, analogous to the role Rome played in the spread of Christianity, but America's spiritual destiny could be thwarted by the Satanic forces of Godless communism.

I was deeply involved in these rallies and demonstrations, which were in direct contrast to the student unrest I had experienced earlier at Harvard. I had been invited to enter the Unification seminary when it opened at Barrytown in 1975, but I postponed it while working in the field on the Unification witness to a spiritualized America. My two years in the seminary were not exactly a retreat from the busy world, but it opened up for me a whole wide world of knowledge that was very different from all the college courses I had had in the physical sciences. I realized that my relatively simple and innocent profession of faith in the theology of Divine Principle was a prelude to deeper intellectual understanding of Christian theology. The complexity of scriptural and doctrinal debates over the centuries required greater intellectual effort than the study of physical sciences.

It was during this time too that I got a deeper appreciation of the theology of both celibacy and marriage. One of the other struggles in my earlier life had been my very ambivalent feelings about sexuality. In my sexual experiences before I met the Church, I had always felt dissatisfied and unfulfilled. I realized that I was just using the other person, being very selfish about it, or the woman was using me. I never experienced a deep love relationship with anyone. Because of that frustration and exasperation it was relatively easy for me to accept the Unification interpretation of the Fall of Man. I could see that the doctrine was true in my own life, and I could accept the theory and practice of a chaste preparation for marriage. Before joining the Church I had begun to

despair that I would ever find the right person to marry
because I had had some unsuccessful relationships. I
also saw so many of my friends' marriages just fall
apart. I was still young enough, in my early twenties,
so I didn't really confront the prospect of marriage,
but I guess I assumed that in the long run I would get
married.

Along with the acceptance of celibacy comes the
decision to forget about dating and searching for a
spouse. We just simply live as brothers and sisters
without thinking about marriage. I have no confidence
in my own ability to choose a life partner. I just get
very uncomfortable when I see people pairing off exclusively and neglecting other people. Then the day comes
in the Unification Church when you are matched and you
know who your spouse is going to be. In the context of
this mode of operation I believed the stories I've heard
about how these matches work out. I believe God is
indeed working through Reverend Moon at the time of the
matching; that he's thinking of me and wanting to give
me someone who is good for me. So I had no hesitancy,
especially since the woman with whom I was matched is
someone I had really respected. I had worked with her a
few times, and I knew her as a good and faithful person,
so I was very happy.

When I was asked my preference in a bride I said I
wanted a Japanese fiancee, an international marriage
that would help to fulfill the broader Unification concept of family. Actually, however, Reverend Moon chose
to match me with a woman of Chinese background whose
family had moved to America when she was about ten years
old. We do not have many Chinese members. The matching

took place in May, 1979, at the New York center, and we had only a brief conversation before we returned and bowed in acceptance to Reverend Moon. As we went through the Holy Wine ceremony, in the presence of all our brothers and sisters, we were both convinced that we had entered into an eternal divinely blessed commitment.

The indemnity we pay, the sacrifice we make, in the faithful observance of celibacy looks quite different when you know who your future spouse is to be. We were civilly and legally married after the matching ceremony, but Lova and I were separated because we were sent on different missions. It was then much more difficult to be celibate. Before that I had just simply accepted the fact of my celibacy as the normal status of a Unification member. Now we were very much in love and yet we had to remain chaste for three years, until the time of the Madison Square mass wedding, and forty days after that. Now that we are living together in marriage we say prayers of thanksgiving to God not only for this sacred blessing but also for the strength He gave us, to remain chaste during that long engagement period. Since marriage and family are theologically integral to the Unification way of life we feel that we continue under God's protection.

Meanwhile, Reverend Moon granted me the privilege of continuing my education in the fields of theology and scripture studies. After graduating from the Barrytown seminary I enrolled to do graduate work for a master's degree at the Harvard Divinity School. I was fortunate then to be allowed to go on also for the Ph. D. at Harvard. An interesting thing has happened to me over these many years of study. In the first place, I have moved away almost entirely from my early interest in a scientific career. I certainly have a religious calling as a member of the Unification Church, but I also now feel that I have a calling to scholarship. I began to move in that direction in the seminary because I realized that this is where both my interests and my intellectual talents lie. Reverend Moon needs scholars, so I have dedicated myself to a scholarly career. At the seminary I did a lot of work with the conferences sponsored by the International Cultural Foundation, and with the New Ecumenical Research Association, and became acquainted with many professors. This was a kind of academic orientation that turns into the lifetime job of scholarship.

Unification scholarship is evolving as a logical consequence of the Barrytown Theological Seminary. More than thirty graduates of the classes of 1977, 1978 and 1979 were assigned to study for doctoral degrees at some of the best universities of the country. Even while we were still graduate students we regularly participated as discussants, and more and more as lecturers, in frequent conferences explaining the Unification movement. Most of the participants were academic and religious professionals with whom we engaged in friendly but critical dialogue.

Out of these experiences of discussion and study we are evolving, developing and refining the theological system of the Unification Church. Our scholars are gaining recognition as intellectual representatives of the Church, engaging in research and writing, as well as lecturing. The body of knowledge known as Unification theology is taking its place in the academic world.

VII

GERTRUDE — LEARNING TO PRAY

I think my earliest experiences with God came to me when I was at Mass in the Catholic Church. As a child I wanted to imitate the women I saw praying in the Church. I was trying to develop the special feeling I thought they had, and just being in the Church itself with Mass going on had an effect on me. My mother was Protestant and not of much religious help. I did not go to a parochial school, but I attended catechism class and went to Church every Sunday until I was about fifteen or sixteen. The trouble is that I never learned how to pray. Nobody gave me such close attention where I could feel the person next to me was experiencing God and helping me to feel that as well on a one-to-one basis. I wasn't getting it at home, obviously. We didn't have prayer life in our family.

Until I went to college most of my friends were Catholics, and I had good relations with people in several youth groups. We talked about everything except God and religion. It seems to me that my experience was the opposite of what I hear from other Moonies who used to be Catholics. They say that a personal relationship with God in the life of prayer was emphasized in their religious training. It was a matter of one-on-one with God, praying for their own salvation without much attention to others. Now they learn a kind of universal love, a real sense of community, among the brothers and sisters of the Unified Family. Knowledge of the Divine

Principle and experience in the movement developed a
universalism of salvation in place of a particularism
for each one's own salvation.   In my own case I went in
the other direction.   I appreciated community solidarity
long before I met the Moonies, but it was only with them
that I learned about prayerful personal relationship
with God, an inner spiritual experience.

What I'm saying here makes it sound as though I
were a deeply religious person and that I was always
searching for God.   Nothing could be further from the
truth.   I hadn't been near a church for years, although
I did study courses in religion as a minor to my
academic major of social work.   Even when I heard my
first Unification lecture I was more interested in race
relations and in world unity than in religion.   I was a
senior at the University of Vermont when I saw a poster
on a telephone pole.   Someone had drawn a picture of
people of different races standing in a circle and
holding hands.   I thought that was really interesting
because I had traveled in Europe the year before, and I
enjoyed meeting people of different cultures.

This was the kind of topic that usually drew crowds
of students on campus whenever such lectures or movies
were advertised.   The sponsor on the poster was the One
World Crusade, and when I went down the hallway it was
so quiet that I thought I was in the wrong building.   I
finally found the room where there were only five
people.   When I looked in they turned around and
everyone smiled.   I excused myself and said "I must be
in the wrong place," but they assured me that this was
the right location.   So I listened to the lecture on the
Principle of Creation given by a young woman who was not

a good speaker and was not really prepared to answer
questions.

They described themselves as members of a One World
Crusade, promoting the unity of all mankind, but did not
identify themselves as the Unification Church movement.
Actually, this first lecture was not very interesting,
and I declined their invitation to come for another one.
A couple months later a female student came up to me on
campus and asked me if I believed in God. She was a
bright girl who made a lot of sense in the reasonable
way she talked about herself, her experiences, and her
religious beliefs. We must have talked for two hours,
while she explained what the Unification movement was
trying to do. This started me off on a point I had
never really considered before in my life. Suppose it
is true, I thought, that God not only exists but is
personally concerned about me, that he has a definite
purpose for me at every moment of my life. I think my
main emotion was that I was scared.

At first the group didn't have a center there in
Burlington, but by the time I really got interested in
their ideas they had established one. I went there
about twice a week, had dinner with them, listened to
their speeches, and carried on long discussions. They
always prayed over the dinner, and that was my first
experience of people praying with each other and out
loud. Certainly I never had that in my own family at
home. I started to get used to the idea of prayer. I
also asked a lot of questions when they gave talks about
their sacred scripture, the <u>Divine</u> <u>Principle</u>. I could
resonate with the universality of their ideas. These
people apparently had very profound experiences with

God, and they helped me to get past a lot of my own fears and resentments and conflicts. Here is where I did find that God is my loving parent, and his presence was a personal experience for me.

The concept of a parental God was a new idea to me. The emphasis on God as a concerned and loving father is very different from the picture of a great judge who ultimately separates the sheep from the goats, and sentences us either to eternal reward or to everlasting punishment. I'm not sure that I ever had a clear notion about God, but I had believed that our own behavior would bring the judgment of God on us and that we were personally responsible for avoiding bad conduct. Perhaps in my earlier years I tended to avoid God, and now I began to see him as a parent who wants us to approach him. Another point that became clear was the realization that I had never really believed in the divinity of Jesus, even though that was supposed to be a Catholic doctrine. How redemption was to come through the death of Jesus was another one of my early vague doubts. I realized now that much in the world was left yet to be redeemed.

I was deep in my books as a college senior in the fall semester of 1972, and also into a lot of extra-curricular activities. I was on the tennis team, and had a large role in a campus movie being made by the drama department. The Moonies would constantly come by and quietly prod me to come over to their house. They were always so nice and friendly that I did not think of them as pests, but they were steadily pursuing me. I was involved in a lot of things on campus but I did become the object of witnessing, that is, a one-on-one

situation where I successively heard all the lectures of
Divine Principle. I was also taking a college course in
the history of Christianity, and had a lot of discussions with the campus chaplains of the different
denominations. I think I went once to the Newman Club,
but I was more interested in the other religious groups
because I had been raised a Catholic. I also attended
services in the different churches around Burlington. I
felt that I was on a spiritual journey, and I wanted to
make all the stops before coming to the end. I reached
my destination when I moved into the Unification center
in January, 1973.

I found another roommate to share the apartment
where I had been living when I moved into the Church
center. My life continued to be very busy in the spring
semester, even though I had only one work-study seminar
a week. I was doing field work in a low-income housing
project for the elderly and could translate this social
work into the kind of human service the Church promoted.
In the evening I would come back to the center and pray
with the members, have dinner, and sometimes go out
fundraising. I remember also that after one week in the
Church you were expected to go out witnessing. I was
nervous about that and very unsure of myself. The first
time, I sat in the coffee shop for three hours before I
had the courage to talk about God to strangers.

Later that year Reverend Moon came through on a
lecture tour, and I had the privilege of meeting with
him in a very small group. He was anything but the
quiet reserved person I had anticipated would be the
model of God's messenger. It was a brief encounter with
the other members present and not a personal

conversation. I would get to know him better later on as a seminarian. The Burlington center was growing, so two other members and I went to pioneer a new Church center in Montpelier, the capitol of Vermont. I had the responsibility of organizing it and finding the funds to keep it going, because at that time every operation had to support itself. I stayed there about six months and then turned it over to another member.

It was about that time that the whole church seemed to be on wheels. Almost everybody was on the road, either as itinerant workers (I.W.) or in mobile fund-raising terms (MFT) or just probing into new towns and cities in search of membership. I did some witnessing to new members in the Boston area, and then spent some time in New Hampshire. In Maine I became part of the staff to run a 21-day workshop. It is obvious that we are given a lot of responsibility right away when we join the Church, even if we feel we are not quite ready for it. In Maine, in January of 1975, two of my sisters became members of the Church.

My father reacted almost violently when my sisters joined me in the Unification movement. At first I had no problems with my parents, who seemed to think this was a passing fancy of mine. And there was no real negative publicity against us at that time. They began seriously to look into the Moonies when my sisters joined and when Ted Patrick and his thugs began to kidnap our members. One of my friends in the Church was kidnapped and forced to recant her religion. She became an anti-Moonie and got the deprogrammers interested in contacting my parents who began to associate with other parents in anti-Moon groups, reading the literature, watching propaganda movies about us. I started getting frantic phone calls from my parents, demanding that we come home.

My father was negotiating with the deprogrammers to have us kidnapped, but my mother was very much opposed to such drastic action. There was apparently a great heated debate in my family. My youngest sister, who was still in high school, was an observer of this domestic controversy, but she kept out of it. My father is Catholic and my mother Protestant, but they did not make their objections from a religious perspective. My father's argument was that Reverend Moon was a charlatan who had duped all these young people. I was pioneering in Louisiana, and my sisters were in Maine, and the phone calls were more frequent that we come back to New Jersey for a family confrontation. My father actually believed that we three college-educated women couldn't think for ourselves. It is a very strange experience to have a conversation with someone who thinks you don't have your mind there and you are not really capable of following a discussion.

This was a very difficult experience, because we had always been a close-knit and loving family. My parents were proud of their four daughters, provided more than adequately for our material needs and educational opportunities. My father was a successful lawyer and very much involved in politics. I can only guess at his motivation, but I think he felt embarrassed that all his important colleagues knew his daughters were Moonies. It was a very confusing and intense period to try and sort out what do do. The Church was trying to protect us against being deprogrammed; and my parents were trying to convince us to leave the movement.

My father was an expert attorney who knew how to argue a case, but he would not listen to the other side of the case. In his mind the Church was the adversary, and nothing good could be said about it. He told us that if we didn't leave the church he would contact every media person he knew, or could find, and tell them this horrible thing that had happened to his daughters - which is exactly what he did. He went to every newspaper editor and television station manager in the New York area, telling them we were the victims of brainwashing. The reporters came around with their cameramen, interviewed us, took pictures and published articles. A large picture of the three of us appeared on the front page of the New York <u>Daily</u> <u>News</u>. We had a big conference with the news media, which appeared on all the major television stations in New York City. The story was reprinted in papers all over the world, even in Africa and Asia.

One of the lessons I learned from this experience is that the news media do not publish a balanced account of the story about religious movements like the Unification Church. The phenomenon of brainwashing is more spectacular, and probably more newsworthy, than the simple fact that an individual has prayerfully converted to a different religion. Members who become apostates after deprogramming are widely publicized, give public confessions to anti-cult groups, and help to kindle hostility against us among our parents. My sisters and I were regularly represented as misguided young women, and our careful explanations of our religious beliefs and practices were dismissed and buried in a deluge of psychiatric terminology. Many otherwise rational people seemed to approve the ritual exorcism practiced on kidnapped Moonies. That year, 1975, was probably the peak of the cynical and negative media coverage of the Unification movement.

In the middle of this controversy I was informed of my acceptance as a student in the first class that entered the Barrytown Seminary in September, 1975. This was also a kind of pioneering experience because it was a new venture for the leaders of the Church, for the faculty and administration of the seminary, as well as for the students. All fifty students were college graduates and felt entitled to further academic credits for graduate study in this professional school. The seminary applied for accreditation, was visited by an evaluation team that gave unqualified approval of this educational institution. It was a routine procedure that coincided with a public hearing about cultism before Senator Dole's committee in Washington in February, 1976. The findings were the basis of attacks against the Unification Church. The New York State senate asked the Board of Regents to "delay" the seminary accreditation. Two years later the Regents formally denied the request for accreditation. Another, the double, rejection came to us when the Church was refused membership in both the New York Council of churches, and the National Council of churches of Christ.

One of the great benefits I experienced at Barrytown was the frequency of Reverend Moon's visits to the seminary. Until then I did not have a secure feeling about him. I did not understand him, and I was vaguely scared of him because he was obviously from a very different culture. The history of his hardships fascinated me, and the way in which the movement was growing all over the world, the manner in which he humbly accepts attacks on him and on the Church - all of this was very impressive. It also convinced me that his spirituality has very deep roots. We all used to go fishing with him in the Hudson River, and on occasion he would stay up all night with some of the students, making and repairing fish nets. I was not keen on working all night so I'd go to bed, but I felt guilty about that. Here was a man who has had great influence on my life and I should be spending time with him, getting to know him.

On one of those nights I had a dream and saw him chuckling at me. He was saying "I have plenty of help; we don't need you to help with the nets. I just want to give you a chance to know me." I woke up from the dream with a wonderful warm feeling about him. I went back to sleep but woke in the morning with a strep throat and 104 temperature. Three days later my throat was better and I went down to the river bank to net fish with him and a handful of seminarians. The others were getting tired because his schedule was so rigorous. From then on I helped regularly whenever he was on the campus. Every time we are with him we get very little sleep. He is constantly talking and counselling and being with the Church members, with very little time for himself and his family. He practices what he preaches: you sacrifice yourself for the world, and you place the world before your family. In order to love your family you have to love God first. There is deep sincerity in his actions and in his beliefs, and the members of his family love him dearly.

When we graduated from the seminary in 1977 the whole class was assigned to the National Mobile Fundraising Team, which occupied us all summer in different parts of the country. This was a special and high-powered campaign, but not a new experience because we had all done fundraising at various times before and since that summer. Reverend Moon always speaks in high praise of the seminary graduates, and he selected a number of us to study for doctorates at some of the big Universities like Chicago, Harvard and Columbia. Among the other graduates he chose some, including me, to be State leaders of the Church. Only five of the State leaders at that time were women; a year later there were only two of us. Then the other sister left to join her husband, and for a while I was the only female State leader.

During the next four years I administered our State center at Huntington, West Virginia. This was a fairly routine job, in which we carried out the normal programs of workshops and lectures, and also introduced a series of new members to the tasks of witnessing and fundraising. Several times a year I was assigned to the conferences sponsored by the Church for the edification of educational and religious leaders. Some of them were seminars, introductory and advanced, to expound the doctrines and practices of the Church. I was called upon to give lectures about the <u>Divine</u> <u>Principle</u>. Another type of conference provided opportunities for scholars to discuss theological questions of great significance to religion and society, but often only

indirectly related to the Unification Church.   In such
instances I helped to organize and manage details of the
program.

   The largest matching in the history of the Church
was scheduled for May, 1979, at the World Mission
Center.   I had been in the Church for six years, had
fasted and prayed with some regularity, and I knew that
marriage was my life's vocation.   I was matched with a
brother whom I knew and admired more by reputation than
by personal contact.   Meanwhile, I was reassigned to
work at Barrytown with the New Ecumenical Research
Association. When we were advised of the date for the
mass wedding at Madison Square Garden in New York we
were also preparing the first Youth Seminar on World
Religions.   Over 150 people arrived at the airport at
the end of June 1982, the day before our wedding.   We
were wildly running around cooperating with several
programs at the same time.   We were doing other conferences around the world that summer, and we did have our
own civil marriage ceremony on 1 September.

VIII

RHINEHART — VISIONS AND IMAGES

My mother died the year before I joined the Unification movement, but her death had nothing to do with my decision. Of course, I missed her because we had always had a close, loving relationship. My father missed her too, but I think he missed more being married, and he soon found himself another wife. Then my father also joined the church, a step to which his new wife strongly objected. That marriage didn't last very long before she divorced him. His next step was to be matched with a Korean member of the Church and to enjoy the blessing of marriage. My brother, who was always jealous of me, also joined the church, but he didn't stay for more than a year. He said he got "tired of it" and walked out.

Life in my family was pretty difficult in my younger years. My father was an authoritarian person, with strong prejudices, but he favored me as his first-born son. He was an accomplished artist and insisted that I too must study art. In fact, I was attending art school in Berlin when I met the Unification movement. We were a traditional Catholic family, and we all went to Sunday Mass together. I attended the middle school when we lived in Oberhausen in the Ruhr Valley, and I went to confession every Saturday until I was about eighteen. In my early years I was very much involved in the activities of the Catholic religion and made close friends with the parish priests.

The strongest influence in my life was certainly my father, whose general attitude toward people and society seemed to me later quite compatible with Moonie teachings. He spoke often about the effects of his war experiences. He was a German patriot and a war hero who felt betrayed when he awakened to the errors of Nazism. He had a nervous breakdown at the time when he was a prisoner of war in Alabama and heard that the Germans lost the war. In a sense I suppose he went through a conversion experience in his ideology. He had been deceived by the fascist system that indoctrinated young people and destroyed individualism for the sake of the mass society. Of course, he was strongly opposed also to the tyranical leftist system of the Communists.

The youth demonstrations of the late sixties and early seventies were reflective of the phenomena that my father most hated. He saw the student protests and strikes of the leftist movements as a kind of parallel to the riotous disturbances on the streets of German cities before the war. He saw the same process of the individual being taken over into some kind of mass identity. In an indirect way I think I picked up my father's resentment of such developments. He remained a war hero but it was as a man of peace that he opposed the extremists, both leftists and rightists. I agreed with him that neither of these ideologies could bring the changes we need for a peaceful world. When the idea of the Messiah was introduced to me in the teachings of Divine Principle I accepted it right away with absolutely no reservations.

In 1971, at the age of twenty, I was at the Art Academy in Berlin, living in what is sometimes called a "Bohemian" style with very little thought of God and religion. One afternoon I was passing the Kaiser Wilhelm Gedachtniskirche in downtown Berlin just as a young lady came out of the Church and we recognized each other. She was from my home town, and I had lost track of her for several years. I invited her for a cup of coffee, but she insisted that I must come with her because she had so much to tell me. I had no intention to do so, because I had an appointment with my girl friend and I didn't want to be late. But she was so enthusiastic about her new experiences and so persuasive in telling them that I went along to the Church center.

It seems she had met the Church in early 1971 and was now a full-time member. As a spiritual condition for success in witnessing to others, she had just finished a seven-day fast and had been saying a prayer of thanksgiving in the Church. So I talked with her and the other brothers and sisters, had dinner with them, and listened to their explanation of the Divine Principle for about three hours. I didn't understand much of it. I went home by subway, but I didn't remember anything of what they said. The next day I went back to learn more about their teachings, and the third day I actually joined the movement.

Meanwhile, my girl friend was unhappy with me because I didn't keep our date. When I told her about my experience with the people at the Unification center she not only forgave me but wanted to hear all about their religious doctrines. The fact that we were in love probably helped this mutual attraction and she too decided to join, and moved into the center. We separated right away, which was the church pattern at the time. It was a real sacrifice to break up this relationship which was emotionally intense. Of course, it meant the end of our sexual relations, but the spirit of religious commitment helped us to overcome these feelings.

The center at Berlin had about fifteen members at the time, was one of the medium-sized groups in Germany, but was considered one of the most successful in witnessing to individuals and lecturing to groups. Paul Werner, the leader of the Church in Germany, was the one who decided to separate us, and he took me with him to the headquarters church, at that time at Essen in the Ruhr Valley. He also happened to be the occasion of an impressive spiritual experience for me. He had been authorized by Reverend Moon to locate and bless some Holy Grounds in Germany. These locations are selected as ideal spots for prayer and meditation, and they are visited with great reverence, somewhat like the shrines that are revered by people in many other religions. There are no buildings or artifacts in these areas, but they are dedicated to the God of nature.

On this occasion I had what might be called a mystical or visionary experience. We stood there at the edge of an open field on a clear cold day. My eyes were opened, and I saw the whole environment change in front of me. The trees were like a large forest that widened into a broad hallway. The scene swayed back and forth as I breathed in and out. I could recognize the brothers and sisters between the trees, and they had a kind of shining image. This was the most enjoyable vision I ever had. After the celebration ended the scene gradually disappeared, and the physical shapes changed back to normal.

I have always believed that the spirit world existed, and I had long accepted the traditional Christian belief in angels and saints. As I associated with Reverend Werner in the next two years there were times when I saw certain spirit men standing next to him. This happened frequently when he was teaching the <u>Divine</u> <u>Principle</u> to an audience. I don't know whether the people there also saw them. I never asked about that. It made a great impression on me at the time. But I never used it as a proof that the spirit world existed; nor did I understand that there was some personal spiritual message intended for me.

The teaching of the Church doctrines was done in the manner of the catechism in those days before we had the printed German version of <u>Divine</u> <u>Principle</u>. One hundred questions had been listed that covered the main points of doctrine, and we learned the given answers. This was not really a study of theology or of salvation history at a scholarly level. The numbers of new members were increasing, and the Church purchased a large training center at Camberg, Taunus. I was with the first group who went there for a 100-day training period, and after that I was myself able to lecture on the main doctrines and practices of the Unification movement. This center was also the stopping place for Unification members from the various European countries.

As soon as we had enough members we spread into the other countries, like Spain, Italy, France, Austria, and

Belgium, and brought back converts, who finished their training and in turn circulated to other countries. Reverend Moon was about to start his 21-city tour across the United States, and I was sent in the first group of over thirty German members to assist in that tour. Others came later, mainly from Germany but some also from other parts of Europe. This was at the end of 1973, and when the tour was over I stayed in America as the director of Camp Asunda, one of the training centers in California. This gave me a first-hand opportunity to improve my use of the English language and to learn about the American way of life. Except for the language it did not seem very different from Germany. Certainly there was a greater similarity between Americans and Germans than between Germans and Orientals, like the Japanese and Koreans.

In June, 1975, I was back in Germany where I was made responsible for the training centers at Neumiller and Tragesmiller. For a while there was a steady flow of new members who kept us very busy in providing the indoctrination for the movement. Then we began to get bad publicity and a certain amount of opposition from groups of parents of our members who were now organizing against the movement. Many times I talked with representatives of these groups, but I succeeded in explaining our movement only when I could speak to two or three at a time. When I tried to address a large audience of them I almost always encountered hecklers who constantly interrupted my speeches. It is not easy to be a messenger from an unpopular religious movement.

It was also about this time that we cancelled the caravans of small teams that had been travelling from city to city. In place of the mobile teams we went as individuals, or as couples, to do pioneering in the smaller towns. We were then called Itinerant Workers, and I must admit that the women members were often more successful than the men in this type of evangelizing. The feminist movement was developing in Germany, which meant that women were expected to be more aggressive than had previously been the case. The Unification sisters had been more numerous than the brothers, from the beginning, and had done much of the evangelizing for new recruits. They do not think of themselves as feminists, nor do we, but they have had some very responsible positions in the movement and are an example of purity and fidelity.

It is customary in the Church to shift directors and leaders from one center to another. In 1977 I was assigned to be leader at our center in Munich, where we made special efforts to increase the number of members. As a matter of fact, the rate of recruitment was slowing down. It appears that our enemies were waging an effective campaign against us. Polemical attacks were instigated from some of the traditional clergy, and their allegations were being repeated in the newspapers and magazines. In all fairness I think that the objectivity of the news media, including newscasts on television, seemed to be slanted against us. We had to respond to such attacks, and I was asked to accept the position of director of public relations at Frankfurt, which had become our national headquarters.

Then in May, 1978, I was invited by Reverend Moon to be matched in the same group with other couples in London, and the blessing took place in the same week.

My wife was a Korean sister who had worked in several European countries, but I had met her only casually with no inkling that we would ultimately be chosen as spouses by Reverend Moon. As is the custom in the Unification Church, the consummation of our marriage was postponed for several years. We both worked out of the Frankfurt center but lived in separate residences.

In the growing storm of antagonism, and in the decreasing rate of recruitment, it was obvious that we had to move in our own defense. This means not only the refutation of the many false charges made against us, but also the public presentation of our positive belief system. We therefore set up an office of public relations in Frankfurt where another brother focused on the news media, while I paid most attention to the churches and the universities. I worked out a careful plan for meeting with representatives in each of the Catholic dioceses of the country. We were cordially received at the first two dioceses on the list, at Osnabruck and at Muenster. I was encouraged that we could discuss our movement in a reasonable way with responsible Church officials. We had appointments with the diocesan representative at Wurtzberg and at Fulda, but unexpectedly got registered letters cancelling these appointments and declaring that an official policy had been established not to have any more conversations with us.

I cannot help but remark that the Catholics have been much more ready to dialogue with the Marxists than with us or with the other young Christian movements. The Catholic papers and publicists have shown no love for us, but they don't express the kind of hostility we get from these other church sources. Of course, we have a lot of members like myself who had been raised and trained as Catholics but are no longer active in the church. We got unfavorable publicity when some seminarians, both in Germany and France, left the Catholic seminary to join the Unification movement. The most publicity came when an Austrian priest, Heinz Kretchek, announced his intention to join our Church. He was well-known as the director of the Catholic youth movement in Austria, and I suppose his reputation suffers even more because he was matched by Reverend Moon and now lives in a blessed marriage.

This kind of happening does not endear us to either the Catholic authorities or to the active Catholic laity, and I do not know how such widely publicized conversions can be made palatable to the church that loses some of its members. There was a time in Germany when tremendous excitement, and much animosity, occurred over the conversion of an important Catholic to Lutheranism, or an important Lutheran to Catholicism. Religious conversions across denominational lines used to be the occasion of hard feelings among the faithful, but the bitterness of such experiences is no longer expressed except in the case of our Unification converts or of other youth religions. It is my hope that the spirit of ecumenism may be extended also to embrace us. I understand that in Italy the Vatican is preparing for conferences along these lines. One scholar of comparative religions in Milan, who has done a lot of research on the Unification Church, has issued invitations for a preliminary meeting. It may not turn out to be as successful as we want it to be, but I am sure it is not going to be the kind of disaster that the Protestants have brought upon us.

Meanwhile, we continue to be under systematic attack from Protestant churchmen like Pastor F. W. Haack and his colleagues, who are making the most outrageous statements about us. They are personally the most vocal of the Church opponents, but are really acting as the official spokesmen of the Lutheran Church in Bavaria, or of one hostile segment of the Church. So it is really a powerful wing of the German Protestant Church that is providing the funds to support their persecution of the new religious movements. If they had goodwill the churches could quickly decide to cut their financial support of these clergy, or could tell them to apply another ethic in dealing with us. In place of the persecution they could start a dialogue with the people in the new religious movements, or at least try to understand them in an ecumenical way. In my opinion they now have a fixed official policy against us, and these attacks are not simply the work of a few bigoted clergymen.

The so-called free churches, like the Mormons and Jehovah's Witnesses, who had been persecuted under Hitler, are not subject to the kind of attacks that are made against us and the other youth religions. Nowadays they are loosely associated with the mainline Evangelische or Lutheran Churches but are not considered equal in any ecumenical dialogue that goes on. For instance, they are still the object of commentaries on new religious movements published by the Evangelische Centrale fur Weganschauungs Fragen in Stuttgart. This is an official institution established by the Protestant Church in Germany to keep watch over these developments. They are very definite in the rejection of the Unificationists. Their attitude toward us is less

vicious than that of Pastor Haack or Pfarrer Hauth, but
I would not call it an ecumenical dialogue.

One of the effects of so much adverse publicity
seems to be an increase of associate members, even while
we have reached a plateau of the core membership. We do
not have the previous large number of young people who
were ready to make a total life commitment to the
Church, but we are attracting more mature people, some
of them married and with children, willing to
participate in the Church. I think many of them have
been contacted through the extended application of the
home church practice. They see our members ready to
give selfless service to their neighbors and without any
compensation. I foresee the establishment of small
autonomous groups around the country who will tithe and
evolve into something like the typical church
congregation or parish.

IX

EUGENIE — HESITANT JOINER

My father died when I was an infant, and my aunts told me later that he had a Catholic burial. My mother declared herself an agnostic, but she did not want to feed me with her own ideas about church and religion. She wanted me to be able to make my own choice in this regard, so she sent me to Mass and to catechism class each Sunday for two years, between the ages of nine and eleven. I had two aunts, my father's sisters, who were very Catholic, very religious and admirable people. My mother would drop me off at their house so that they could take me to church every Sunday. That was the extent of my relationship with organized religion. After a while I consciously made the decision not to have any further relationship.

If you grow up in Puerto Rico, as I did, you cannot completely ignore the Catholic Church, but an interesting thing happened to me that I later recognized as the difference between religion and spirituality. The Church was strong and visible and organized; there were nuns and priests; there were processions and sacraments and Mass and confession, but there wasn't any particular feeling for Jesus, for God. I am not blaming anybody for this. It was the way I experienced it, and it was only later that I noticed the absence of any deep spiritual contact with God. I remember that as a young teenager in high school I spent a lot of time observing

nature and observing people. I wrote a paper as a
junior in high school, in which I concluded that nature
itself was God.

I always had a deep respect for human beings -
which is why I became a sociologist - and I tried to
understand why people behave the way they do. Puerto
Rico is a society that is multi-cultural but with the
different social classes living in close vicinity. It
wasn't the rich watching the poor from a distance, and
vice versa. I tried to build good, healthy, wholesome
relationships with everyboy, boy friends, my family,
students and teachers, men and women in general. So the
question of love became important, and ultimately that
led me back to the question I had left behind, which was
the question of God. I'm not sure I understand this
myself. Unificationists would probably say it was God's
guidance. I'm a Unificationist. I believe it was
partly God's guidance, but also that this was just
happening in my life.

My first two years in college were at Centenary
College for Women in New Jersey - not the big one in
Louisiana - but then I moved north to do the junior and
senior years at the University of New Hampshire. I took
some courses in comparative religion but did not pay
attention to Christianity or to any of the various
Christian churches. I was trying at that point to learn
as much as I could about the Eastern religions. I took
courses in Oriental philosophy and immersed myself in
Zen and Yoga, and even practiced the meditations
promoted around the campus by Buddhists and Hindus.
There was even a small group who called themselves the
Human Potential Movement. I heard about the Unification

movement for the first time in my senior year when a friend phoned and said, "I have met these remarkable people. You should too."

The remarkable people he met sat around at the Student Union building on the university campus, willing to talk with anyone who would listen, and inviting students to attend lectures. The University allowed them to use a room for these lectures, open to the public and given with some frequency. I sought them out and asked them to teach me what it was they were teaching everyone else. This was not a case where they came after me and witnessed to me. Maybe that's why it took me so long to join up. At that time, in the winter of 1973, Church was much smaller than it is now. The campus lecture was the main format, but they also invited me to their house for dinner. During the last semester of my senior year I went to several workshops where I stayed overnight on weekends. I was not ready to make a commitment because there were other options I was sampling.

At the same time I was very serious about studying the Eastern religions and associating with people who were both the Maharishi Yogi group and the 3HO, or Healthy-Happy-Holy Organization. I would do my yoga with them in the morning and then in the afternoon go off by myself and read the Bible. The communal things I did were the meditations with these students, but I remember desperately trying to understand the words of Jesus. I became a vegetarian at that point as part of my external way of trying to purify what I felt was inside of me. I had many friends who were part of this new wave of young people who were changing their external behavior, their clothing and hairstyle and their general appearance.

My mother and my sister came for graduation in May, 1973. They were horrified at my appearance, straggly hair, no make-up, wearing Indian clothes. With my vegetarian diet, my physical looks had changed. They said I was emaciated. They tried not to be directly critical of my attitudes, but they certainly expressed concern about my health and my appearance. I could just tell that I was isolating myself from them. At that point the Unification Church was not in the picture. I had made no commitment, and I had nothing to say to them about that. The fact is that I had not been close to my family for a long time and we were almost strangers. To this day I have regrets that I did not make some effort to embrace them and to show them that I loved them. I was moving toward a spiritual solution of the problems I saw in the world, and my family members were in no way religious. Perhaps they would not have understood.

The fact is that I was having difficulty with Unification theology, and I decided to shelve it while I signed up with the VISTA program (Volunteers In Service To America). I was sent to work among the Mexican-Americans in Corpus Christi, where my ability to speak Spanish was a real advantage in teaching elementary schoolchildren. It was the story of my life in repetition. I had gone to the University for a degree in sociology, to seek the answers to world problems, and I came up with spirituality. Then I got into the practical work of the VISTA program, using my social work training, attempting to help these people with methods and knowledge and techniques. But I came to realize that I was not providing fully for their needs. So I went back to meditation and yoga, and my vegetarianism became even more stringent.

My religious search continued. I had made a pledge to God that I would visit a Christian denomination every Sunday and then make a decision of which church to join. The priority in my life was to find some answers to the deep spiritual and theological questions. So I went to a different service every Sunday and heard sermons by Baptist, Lutheran, Methodist, Episcopalian, and other preachers. I was doing my own experiences of the Eastern faiths, fasting and meditating. I think this process began as a child with a sincere desire to understand people, and as I grew older it changed to questions involving sociology, philosophy and theology. The Unificationists would say that these were the "conditions" I was setting to make some kind of commitment.

Unexpectedly I got a phone call from the man who had first alerted me to the Unificationists in New Hampshire. He had joined the Church and was a member of the touring New Hope Singers who were now performing in Austin, the State Capital. I had always had deep respect for his commitment to the movement, even while I couldn't agree entirely with their theology. So at his invitation I went up from Corpus Christi to Austin. I knew intuitively that he was going to get me to go to another workshop because that's what they always do. I knew he had that in his mind because every Moonie wants every other person to become a Moonie. So I did attend the weekend workshop, Saturday and Sunday. It was a good opportunity to meet him again and some of the others I had known on the campus.

On the second day I was listening to the Fall of Man lecture, and at that point I had to say honestly that I had a spiritual experience. I have no other rational way of explaining it. I remember the date exactly, June 9, 1974. I was quietly sitting there, when I felt a tremendous wave of warmth and peace coming through me. I blanked out the man and his lecture, and I was thoroughly involved in the physical and psychological experience I was going through. I remember just thinking to myself, "this must be right." At that point, and without the usual struggle like "I've got to leave my job; I've got to leave my family," I peacefully came to the decision: "I must make the commitment." I listened to the rest of the lecture, chuckling to myself because I knew that Jim, like every Moonie, would be elated to find that I had made a commitment. I saw him, had a cup of coffee, and said casually "I guess I should join." Even though that was a serious moment of commitment it didn't seem so serious because I was so happy to make it.

The next step was to return to Corpus Christi, resign from the program and clean up the odds and ends. Within a few days I came back to Austin to join the members in the International One World Crusade that was just about to leave for Oklahoma. This was a quick assignment, and that same day I was in a van travelling to Tulsa. It seemed the natural and logical thing to do, and I did not feel I should clear it with my mother who had by then moved to Massachusetts. My family are very kind and good people, so I did not get the kind of harassment that other members sometimes get from their families. When I went home for Christmas that year they asked me to talk with some minister they knew. That was their way of handling it, and I did it. They are still unhappy about what I did and in some ways their displeasure is painful for me.

Given the kind of friends I had made in my college years I was not seriously alienated from any of them. I still communicate with them. Some of them come to our lectures and make their own decisions about God and religion. Many of them are married and have children, and I enjoy visiting them when I'm in their vicinity. People continue to join the Unification Church, some as full-time dedicated persons, and many others who are simply affiliated with the movement. They accept the ideals of the <u>Divine</u> <u>Principle</u>; their hearts grow and they learn to be ecumenical. They are an influence of love and service in their small communities. But on a much larger scale there is all the work the Unification Church is doing with the academic world and with the religious world.

My close relationship in the Unification community has given me certitude, confidence, faith, that I didn't have before I joined. I had been seeking for an authentic answer in a very uncertain world. Now I have hope in a very profound and meaningful way. In my own case it's a conviction that my life is improving because I know what is happening to me; I know what I've been through. My life is improving and will continue to improve. I keep growing in my triple commitment to <u>Divine</u> <u>Principle</u>, to Reverend Moon and to the Church. They are all one and the same, but they are also

different, even while they are all involved in the
mystery of God. I see a process of growth in myself, in
the confidence that I can become a more loving, more
wise and more considerate person. Beyond that it's a
hope that the world will become a better place and be
improved by the Unification Church.

One of the important aspects of our movement that
outsiders do not understand is that we do not want to be
labeled as a new and different Christian denomination.
Maybe it's too late in America to change the image that
people have of us as a new and separate church. We know
that is not Reverend Moon's message, nor his purpose.
Our task is to revitalize world Christianity, to widen
its embrace so that we include all religions, as well as
all nations and races. The Kingdom of God, toward which
all of humanity is moving, will certainly not be
exclusively for Christians, or Westerners, or
Unificationists. In a sense we are doing in a modern
movement what Jesus intended for all His followers:
that they reach out to all the world. We like to think
that we are redoing His mission and are not starting
something that is brand new out of Korea.

My first year as a Unificationist was spent partly
on the road and partly as State leader in Rhode Island.
I had thought so long and deeply about the teachings of
the Divine Principle that I found it quite simple to
lecture to any interested persons. Witnessing on a one-
to-one basis was a pleasure because I love to talk with
people, and I don't mind walking right up to strangers
and asking them how they are getting along with God.
The fundraising was more difficult from a statistical
perspective; a much higher percentage of people turned

away and refused to donate than the proportion who gave us money. After my visit home at Christmas I was appointed director of our center at Providence, Rhode Island. It was a time when increasing numbers of young people were on the search for God. The responsibility of leadership was lifted when the Barrytown seminary opened and I was accepted as a student.

From that point on I have been involved primarily at the academic level of Unification activities and programs. The seminary is a professional school of theology,and all of the seminarians are graduate students. We were often reminded that our selection for study in the seminary was a signal to prepare for heavier responsibilities in the work of the church. It was suggested that the leadership of the Church in the future was to come from these students. Our courses in Church history, comparative religions, biblical studies, patristics, theological systems, were fairly similar to the program of studies in the better known non-denominational seminaries. Everyone was already fully familiar with the Divine Principle, including the faculty made up of Catholic, Protestant and Jewish professors. In other words, our seminary education branched out much wider than the doctrinal system of the Unification Church.

A special advantage we enjoyed, both as seminarians and as graduate students at several universities, came from the many ecumenical conferences in which we participated. Some of these were held at the seminary, bringing representatives of many churches to discuss central issues of religion. We helped also to conduct expository conferences, both introductory and advanced, of the Unification teachings. These were held in Mexico, the Bahamas, the Virgin Islands, and several European countries. We gave some assistance at the annual International Conference of the Unity of Sciences (ICUS). It is a very broadening experience to confer with so many expert scholars, learned and religious men and women. The intent of these programs is to influence other people favorably to the church, but a very important effect is what it does for us as individual members of the Church.

Another significant and very personal factor in my life is the Unificationist doctrine and practice on the centrality of marriage and family. One of the reasons I stayed through all the hardships of membership in the church was the anticipation of the matching and marriage. I had finished my work in Rhode Island and was studying at Harvard University when I got the call for the "705 matching ceremony," as we call it, for the number of couples who were designated by Reverend Moon in May, 1979. We were in the large ballroom of the World Mission Center, where Reverend Moon asked who was willing to enter an interracial marriage. I volunteered at that point. My honest sense was that I was going to be quite open, and go by faith. I had the idea that I would marry a black man, and I knew that I could offer this to God and to Reverend Moon. He intimated that it was not correct in my particular case to be matched to a black man. He had stressed to us that day that there is a fine balance between having utter faith in God through his minister, Reverend Moon, but also a strong sense that you take responsibility in accepting or rejecting what is being suggested for you. So, when he suggested that it was not proper for me to be matched to a black person, I took that to be the will of God.

Many of the brothers and sisters at that point were matched across racial lines, black with white, Oriental with white, Oriental with black. Then he asked for members who would volunteer for marriage with a person from another nationality or culture. I waited for the rest of the afternoon, until he asked for all the seminarians and graduate students to come together. He asked us then whether we wanted to marry people who also had college degrees. Did we want to marry State leaders of the Unification Church? It was a very tense moment for us, because we knew that a very important decision was to be made, that involved our personal responsibility and the rest of our life.

This was to be the second great spiritual experience of my life. It was like the moment when I had made the commitment to join in Austin, Texas. Now I had a tremendous confidence in God and in Reverend Moon. I had confidence in myself, that I could make the right decision about this particular suggestion. It was a very peaceful moment, a very happy moment. It all happened very fast. He looked at everyone for a while. He talked with some of the older leaders of the Church; then all of a sudden he started just pointing his finger, saying, "you and you." The man and I looked at each other and smiled. We bowed to Reverend Moon and the elders, and we went up to the balcony where every couple went to talk. I gathered that he knew more about me than I knew about him, and was happy with the choice. I had just an intuitive sense that this is right; this is good. I could see no logical reason to say no.

We went through the Holy Wine ceremony on Mother's Day, which was hilarious because it was not much of a Mother's Day gift for the mothers of some members. Two months later, in July, we took out the marriage license and went through the civil marriage ceremony. Of course, we were not married in the eyes of the Church, so to speak, until the mass wedding at Madison Square Garden in 1982. Being matched while waiting for marriage puts the individual in a new and different status. Unlike other engaged couples who may experiment with premarital sex activities, the Moonie-matched couple remains strictly celibate. Marriage itself is a sacred vocation for which certain preparatory sacrifices are made. We could not pray together about the serious ideals of marriage before we came together to start our family.

X

JOHANN — PUBLIC RELATIONS

When I joined the Vereinigungskirche in 1972 there were only about 120 members in the Federal Republic of Germany. That seemed a very slow growth since the time when the first missionaries came from the United States in 1963. It is a peculiar fact that the Unification movement came from Korea to Germany by way of California. One of Reverend Moon's earliest disciples, Young Oon Kim, who was fired from the faculty of Ewha Women's University in Seoul, went as his missionary to America in 1959. Among her converts on the West Coast were several German immigrants, among them Peter Koch and Ursula Schumann who returned to their native land in 1963 as the first missionaries to this country.

Peter Koch was a very spiritual and hard-working man who set up special conditions for the European Church. He fasted for forty days when he established modest headquarters in an apartment in Frankfurt. In the following year he made his first German convert but had the foresight to incorporate legally as a registered association (eingetragener Verein). As he gained a few more converts he sent them almost immediately as missionaries to establish centers in Austria, France and Spain. Most of these early members were in their late thirties and early forties, much more mature than the many younger members who became known as a youth religion. There is a sense in which we can say that Germany was the mother Church of the European

Unification movement, although an American, Doris Orme, was largely responsible for establishing the Church in England.

By the time I met the Church there were already thirty small centers in Germany, one of them in Essen where I was first approached on the street by two members who asked me what was my purpose in life. This was in early 1972 when I had many other things on my mind, especially my education for a career in the business world. But this meeting was a deep and disturbing experience because I suddenly realized that they were talking about God. I am not sure why this awakened an unexpected response in me, unless it was by the divine spirit. I called myself a religious person, a believer in the existence of God, but I hesitated to call myself a Christian. I was raised in a Catholic family, and I had taken catechism lessons about religion and God and church, but I had a feeling that if I called myself a Christian I would have to live up to the beliefs of the religion. Some of the doctrine I couldn't accept, for example, the eternity of Hell as taught to me by my Catholic Sunday school teachers.

It seemed to me a good idea then to try to learn more about religion, and I began to attend evening conversations about the Divine Principle. They were one-on-one dialogues about the doctrine, and I wanted to keep a certain distance and not get involved directly with the group. It was only after hearing the whole doctrine that I got to meet and talk with more of the members. Then I was invited to dinner several times and learned about their aspirations for converting the whole world. During that time I was still living with my family and continuing my educational training in business management. I was serving my apprenticeship, or doing fieldwork as the Americans call it, with the Coca-Cola Company. There is nothing more American than that. After three months I asked my parents' permission to move into the church center, which I then did.

Moving into the church center constituted my commitment to the Unification movement, and I was then a full-time member but only a part-time participant. They encouraged me to complete my training in business administration. On the side, so to speak, I was learning how to witness to people about the teachings and practices of the Church. So, during that period of about eight months I would occasionally travel around with one of the caravans, which were missionary teams of four or five members going into different cities where we had small Church centers. Now it's completely different. We have big Church centers everywhere, and we don't use caravans any more.

Toward the end of the year there was much talk about sending a big group of European missionaries back to America. It was an invitation rather than an assignment, but I was reluctant to accept it because I did not like America. I didn't want to go there, and I had hoped to go and work with the Church in Asia. It took me some time of thinking before I decided I should join the large group of seventy brothers and sisters going over to be with Reverend Moon on his first Day of Hope tour. He started this 21-city tour in New York with a speech at Carnegie Hall. It was a terribly hard time during those first weeks because I didn't speak much English. We were out on the street almost all day, selling tickets to the lecture and the festival. On the average each member sold about two tickets a day, but the leaders finally decided to give the tickets away free of charge. I personally had very little visible success in this effort, but I did have many deep spiritual experiences.

My personal contact with Reverend Moon himself precipitated these experiences. He had come to Essen several years before I joined the movement, when he gathered sixty members from all over Europe for a kind of summit conference. He appointed Paul Werner as leader of the German Church and assigned Peter Koch to replace Werner in Austria. But the most exciting event of that visit in 1969, which got some newspaper publicity, was the matching and public wedding of eight German couples. He came again in 1972, and I met him personally just three weeks after becoming a member. He had completed a seven-city tour in the United States, had visited the members in Britain and given some lectures there. The speech in Essen on this occasion was his first public appearance in my country. Several other developments are worth noting. The decision was made to begin fundraising for the first time by selling literature on the streets. Also, for the first time we had available the printed German translation of Gottliche Prinzipien. Up to that time we had been using the mimeographed translation done by Peter Koch.

The members of the Church recognize a charismatic quality in Reverend Moon, and he is revered as a specially chosen vicar of God the Father. I was a neophyte when I first talked with him in Essen, and I found him very lively and friendly as he chatted informally with us. Perhaps I expected some kind of mystical experience, but I didn't have any definite feeling about him. Oddly enough, in spite of my reluctance to go to the United States, I vaguely thought that some special spiritual event would happen. Nothing unusual occurred, and all my earlier experiences then built up in a feeling of frustration.

When we had this first evening in Carnegie Hall on 1 October, 1973, I was sitting in the front row. We had distributed many tickets, in fact three times as many as there were seats. I was quite surprised by that because I had the feeling that we would be overcrowded, that there would not be enough space for all the people trying to get in. Reverend Moon had told us that usually only about one-third of the ticket-holders show up. In this case not even enough came to fill the hall, and I again felt frustration. I thought this man, Reverend Moon, who put his energy and his whole heart into this crusade tour would also feel disappointed. But he wasn't, and I was very touched by his attitude of confidence which was so different from mine.

Later I had other experiences as I was praying and wrestling to find the heart of God. I remember one time I was driving on the interstate highway in Florida, and I passed an old black woman standing by the side of the road and holding a sign, "To Cleveland, Ohio," which was quite a distance from there. I just began to meditate about her. Why is she there all alone? What is she going to do? Where are her children? Was she going to her family in Cleveland? Where will she sleep that night? Suppose nobody stops to give her a ride? Suddenly I began to imagine that she symbolizes God who is willing to go through all difficulties to meet His children. The same questions can be asked about His relationship to us. For a moment I thought to go back, pick her up and drive her to Cleveland; but I didn't do that. So, there were key moments like this that made me realize more deeply how God is acting in my life.

During the first four months in America I was together only with those who had come from Germany for the crusade with Reverend Moon. Then during the whole year of 1974 I was the only German in a team of about sixty members. There were twenty Japanese, twenty French people, ten Italians and Americans, and some other nationalities. I was appointed assistant leader of this international team, and I had a lot of administration work taking care of the many details of travel activities. I reached out to many strangers and brought them to attend the festivals and the lectures of Reverend Moon, which I felt to be very valuable. Because we were moving from place to place around the country I could not invest myself long enough in any individual to bring that person into the Church. So, at this point I was not providing spiritual children for the movement.

It was in the same year, 1974, when Reverend Moon was already permanently established in the United States, that he formed the first truly global, or inter-national, crusade. He called in more than 150 members from twenty-five nationalities. These were the Western Unificationists who were now going back to Asia, whence there had already come the revered prophet of Korea. I went with these missionary teams to spend eight months in Japan and three months in Korea. The Westerners worked with their Asian brothers and sisters, learning enough of the foreign language to engage in witnessing to the faith. Witnessing in any language is always more difficult than fundraising, and it is spiritually more rewarding. You have to reach out to the people, trying to understand them personally to reach their heart. With goodwill and hard work we were able to penetrate the cultures that are foreign to us, but witnessing is more successful with your own compatriots.

At the end of 1975 I returned to Essen to spend a few weeks with my family. This relationship with my parents was always warm and happy. They never placed any obstacle to my vocation as a Unificationist. They had given their permission and blessing when I originally moved into the center at home, and we continued contact through letters and sometimes phone calls. They and I find it difficult to understand why there is so much antagonism and so much bad press about "breaking up families." I think in America my mother and father would be called "Moonie Parents." They have attended lectures and seminars and social programs sponsored by the Church and seemed to enjoy meeting many of the sisters and brothers. They are very modern Roman Catholics who caught on to the ecumenical spirit of denominationalism.

It seems to me that most German parents of our members get along well with their children, or at least learn to accommodate the new relationship. But there have been exceptions. In 1975 a small group of parents, with the help and advice of some clergymen, organized in opposition to the new youth religions. They did not resort to abducting the children for deprogramming,

which was strictly illegal under the federal protection
of religious freedom. But there was one notorious
instance of a young German who joined the church in
California. His parents went over to the States with
some ex-Moonies, hired an American deprogrammer, kidnapped their son and detained him until he apostatized. He
later published an article, "I was a Moonie," but admitted that he had at least found Christianity in the
Unification Church.

I think that one of the big differences between us
and the Americans is that we do not have large numbers
of publicity-seekers among the ex-members who tell
horror stories about their life in the Church. As far
as I know, only in America is there this phenomenon of
hatred and anger on the part of deprogrammed ex-members
who turn viciously against their former brothers and
sisters. There are probably over two hundred German
former members, and most of them speak kindly of their
Church experience, like my sister-in-law, who was even a
foreign missionary but is now going a different way. We
all know Klaus Linder who was matched and married by
Reverend Moon, and left the Church in 1980 while being
supported with Church funds as a graduate student at
Harvard University. He published a fairly objective
theological criticism of the Divine Principle under the
title, "Cultural and Semantic Problems in the Study of a
New Religion." He did not exhibit personal bitterness
or rancor.

The Church was steadily gaining more members in
Germany, but the development of the German Church is
something special because we always send so many
missionaries to foreign countries. We soon learn that

we are an international church. Often we are sent out in groups, and even in a world crusade like in 1975, and sometimes we go as individuals to work in the centers already established in other countries. For example, after visiting my family I was working three months in France, and three months in Italy. Then I came back in the summer of 1976 and was appointed as leader of the Church center in Berlin. This assignment kept me there for two very busy years while the church continued to expand in membership and in activity programs. The Church was beginning to come under attack by critical journalists and especially by hostile clergymen, as well as by politicians and government agencies.

The Church leaders decided that we had to work to improve our public relations, and they set up a special office for this purpose in Frankfurt. I was appointed the first director of this program, and have made this my special vocation within the Church. We had never had a press officer, or public relations spokesman, so I didn't know where to start. I could call myself a trained business administrator, but I had to find my way through this new profession. I read through all the newspapers, and get many negative and hostile reports about the Unification Church. My job is to offset these attacks, but you can't be naive. Often a news reporter comes and tells me, "I'm not really much of a friend of the Moonies, but at least I want to treat you fairly. So, please give me some information, and I will write an objective report." There is a human tendency, especially among the Moonies, to trust people, to believe in their goodness, but if you treat openly with journalists like that you might run into some sad experiences.

In some cases the journalists wrote positive reports - I read some of them - but their publishers did not allow them to publish it. That was the case with one of the weekly magazines, Quik. One of their female reporters did a very objective account about the arrival of the International One World Crusade in Germany. Then the editor got someone else to interview a so-called sect expert of the Protestant Church, who provided the usual lot of ex-Moonie stories. That's what got published and nothing else. We did have some sympathetic commentaries, but the whole issue of religion is not as important in Germany as in America. We don't have a First Amendment on which to have public discussions. In Germany we have the two big churches that are financed by the Kirchensteuer collected for them by the government.

The so-called "free churches" do not get financial support from the government, and the so-called cults or youth religions also have to find their own finances. Freedom of religion is guaranteed in Germany, but there has been animosity expressed by agencies of the churches, by social workers, by the Aktion Jugendschutz, and by the government Ministry for Youth, Family and Health. Some of these opponents are making the same kinds of charges that are publicized in the United States: accusations of brainwashing, deception and coercion. The federal government has been interested enough to sponsor an investigation into the new religions, mainly the Children of God and the Unification Church. Unfortunately, public opinion tends to be formed often by the sensationalist press rather than by scholarly reports.

The sociologists at the University of Tubingen conducted research into the youth religions, and did in-depth interviews with me as well as the national leaders of the Church. The field research was done mainly by Dr. Bert Hardin, who published a sociological study of the German Unification Church. Another social scientist, Professor Gunter Kehrer, edited the best known work, Das Entstehen einer neuen Religion, which was exemplified by our church. We have nothing to hide and are always ready to cooperate with responsible investigators of our movement. In some cases we were constrained to take action to offset the slander and public falsehood, as when we brought suit in the Provincial Court of Dortmund against four ministers of the Lutheran Church to enjoin them from spreading vicious propaganda against us.

I am confident that the federal government will find in our favor whenever attempts are made to legislate against us. Already, in 1977 criminal proceedings brought against Paul Werner and the Church members were dismissed as groundless. A more recent and more ambitious proposal had been made that the European Parliament investigate the so-called "new religious movements" within the whole European Community. While the Unification Church is the best known of the movements and the one that has been most frequently attacked, the proposed resolution asks that any individual in any European country be protected from "the machinations of these movements and their physical and moral coercion." The publicity surrounding this initiative brings pressure on actual and prospective members of the youth religions.

One of the interesting results of this broad-based international resolution is that it has brought protests from many of the mainline churches. The rallies that the American church people promoted in support of religious liberty, when Reverend Moon was convicted of tax evasion, are being imitated in Europe not only by German churchmen but also by the French Protestant Federation of churches and by the British Council of churches. We are convinced that the proponents of this initiative want to target certain unpopular "new" religions, but we see a clear danger even to the large established churches of Europe. It is an interesting fact that the churchmen were joined by liberals and communists in opposition to the resolution, on the argument that it is a threat to both religious and civil liberties.

My job in public relations is something more than fighting off the enemies of the Church. I developed publicity for the International One World Crusade (IOWC), that involved over three hundred members. We established four main regions, with concentration on the cities of Frankfurt, Stuttgart, Munich, and Hamburg. The leaders of the different European national churches are responsible for these regions. The British were working mainly in Hamburg and the northern part of the country. The Italians are active in Munich and Bavaria. The leader of the French Church brought his members to the area around Stuttgart. The Austrians are cooperating with the German members around the headquarters of Frankfurt.

In my official position in the Church I am very conscious of the public interest in European unity.

This international objective is in complete harmony with our own goal of unification not only among the religions but also across international and interracial boundaries. Certainly our own members strive for a growing international consciousness, and help to promote the international community among young people. The purpose of this crusade is multiple, not only to promote international friendships and to witness to the truths of religion, but also to gain new members and to dedicate personal service to the needs of neighbors in the home church movement.

The home church is at the grassroots of the whole Unification movement in every country. This is ultimately where our membership of associates will experience the Kingdom of God on earth. The experiments of forty days of pioneering have been accomplished in every country where the Church exists. It is furthest advanced where it has been longest in existence, with the largest number of members. Now that married members are settling down to family life and raising children we begin to see the extension of God's work at the neighborhood level.

XI

MARY — INTERRACIAL MATCH

My first year in college I lived home with my family in Marshall, Texas. We were all good Catholics, except my father who was a wonderful man but he never went to church. The next three years I lived in the women's dormitory of the University of Texas at Austin. I spent a lot of time at the Newman Club, went to confession every other Saturday, and to Mass and communion every Sunday. I've always been interested in religion, because I always wanted to know who God was. I can never remember any point in my life when I did not believe in God. I wanted to know God deeply because I figured that somebody made me, and I had to find out who or what it was that made me.

When I was a college senior I had the job of resident assistant in the dormitory, and one of the girls invited me to a Christian prayer meeting. It seemed that she was always reading the Bible; even at night she would sit in the hallway reading because she didn't want to turn on the light and disturb her roommate's sleep. I was very curious about her dedication to the Bible, and I was glad to go to the prayer meeting. I don't know what it was, but when I was with those students it was the first time in my life that I felt a deep love for Jesus. The way they spoke about Jesus made me feel that He must really be great. It wasn't that I didn't believe in Him before; it was just I felt He was now in my life. I remember that I prayed with them, and I started crying because I was so deeply touched.

It was not long after that I happened to watch a group performing on the campus in front of the Student Union. They were doing what they called the "Celebration of Life," and it included an Oriental Folk Ballet that expressed a bright happy spirit. I asked one of the young men standing there, "does this have anything to do with God?" At first he seemed surprised that I should ask such a direct question, but he said "well, you know, we are the Unification Church." I asked him what that was. He claimed that they wanted to unite all the religions and all the races and all the people of God into one family. That would surely be good news to any black person. The Unified Family was the key term, and it hit me very strongly.

He invited me to dinner at one of the Church centers they had there in Austin. They all seemed to be real nice people, very warm and embracing and friendly, and they treat you immediately like a member of the family. One of the girls who was there was in my class at school, and I didn't even know she was in the Unifi- cation Church. It was nice to see young people sharing in fellowship, so I went over several times but I had no idea of joining their church. It was like the Newman Club, just the feeling of everybody doing something for God, and I thought this was wonderful. It wasn't as though I was getting ready to change from one church to another.

Then they invited me to come to a weekend workshop to hear the religious teachings of their movement.

There were more than fifty members of the Church in town, because they included the travelling troup of the Performing Arts. That workshop was open to the public, so they had to rent a large hall in one of the school buildings. This was a turning point for me - and an important decision. After I heard the explanation of the Divine Principle I knew that I would have to support this movement. What was new to me was the first principle of creation, which talked about God's suffering heart, that He was in pain because He had lost His children, and throughout history he has been working to bring about the Kingdom of God on earth. I think this affected me because I was always close to my own physical father.

My father was a very lovable and loving person, without much education and only moderately successful in his work and income. He was always interested and concerned about us, my older sister, my five brothers, and me. He wanted us to get more education than he and my mother had. So we went to the parochial school, then to public high school, and I was able to attend the State University. The only argument he ever had with my mother, that I know of, was his reluctance to pray and to go to church. Now he seems to be changing. He's talking with the parish priest and beginning to study the Catholic faith.

So the lecture about God the Father touched my heart. Later on, at another workshop I heard Colonel Pak talk in great praise and love of Reverend Moon, and I immediately began thinking about him as a True Parent, as the spiritual father of all the members. As I learned more about him I felt an incredible love for him, like a daughter's love for her father. I think fatherhood was more than just symbolic to me as I experienced it in God the Father, in Reverend Moon as spiritual father, and in my own physical father. If I had to say what convinced me to join the Unified Family I think it was a combination of motives. The first attraction was the loving family spirit of the members; and then the teachings of family and parenthood that I heard in the workshops on Divine Principle.

About a week after the big public workshop I moved into the Church center, and that was with some reluctance. I was attending the summer session after my senior year, to get the two courses I needed for graduation. I was out of the dormitory, and for the first time in my life I had a whole apartment for myself, and I really liked living there. I remember one of the brothers said, "if you move into the center you will have the other members as a support of your faith, and you'll also be able to study more." I knew it was a serious step, and I prayed hard about it. But I did not feel that I was abandoning one religion to enter another. I didn't think of it as a conversion from one church to another. I thought that I had found a fulfillment of the Catholic Church.

So I moved into the Church center and finished my courses in the summer school. My parents came up to visit me one weekend, but they didn't know anything about the Unified Family. They hadn't heard anything negative about it. I explained that I was living in this residence with other young Christians, and that we were the Unification movement which was interdenominational. My mother said that this was even better than living in an apartment by yourself. She was excited about it and felt that it was wonderful. My father liked it too. He talked with the brothers and sisters, and before they went home he told me "these people are very nice."

My parents are simple people. They loved me and trusted me, but in the ensuing years they began to hear terrible stories about Reverend Moon and the Unification movement. When I would come home for visits they were satisfied that I looked all right and acted normally, but they were confused because my relatives told them about brainwashing and how the Moonies were such strange people. They looked at me and said "you look fine to us. You haven't changed for the worse, but we hear so many strange things about your movement." It was pretty difficult for them, because they were struggling to find out what they should believe about us. Their friends would meet them and say, "you poor things. Your daughter was such a nice girl, and now she's in that terrible Unification Church, and she's been brainwashed." My mother would just fall apart and feel ashamed, because she was always so proud of me. She was sensitive to what the relatives said about me, and she tended to believe everything she read in the newspapers. All this didn't faze my father who said he didn't believe anything they put in the newspapers.

The summer of 1975 was an exciting time, because all the members around the country were preparing for the great Madison Square Garden Rally. That brought me to New York for the first time and gave me a better understanding of the national programs of the Church and of the varieties of people who were doing them. I was also able to attend more programs and lectures in that area. For a few months I was fundraising, but I then got into a special kind of vocation. When I was still in Austin I had been inspired by colonel Pak's speech at the Celebration of Lights. I was sitting in the audience and I prayed to God, "Use me in the maximum way that I can testify to your presence to the most people at one time." At the moment I knew that God gave the answer to my prayer: "if you want to testify to me before the most people I will use you in the capacity on stage through the performing medium."

It was later that fall, when I had almost forgotten that spiritual experience, that the music director of the Performing Arts just said to me, "I think you should be in this group." This was the beginning of five years on the road. We toured America back and forth many times. We performed for youth groups, for hospitals and nursing homes, in churches and colleges, singing Christian folk music that was very different from the typical popular rock concerts. The largest crowd I ever sang before was the bicentennial celebration at the Washington Monument in 1976, where there were said to be three hundred thousand people. In 1977 we sang at the closing ceremony of the sixth ICUS, the International Conference on the Unity of Science, in San Francisco.

I was still on tour when Reverend Moon sent out invitations for a matching in 1979. We were always asked our preferences, and I said I'd like to marry an Oriental. There had been interracial marriages in my family before with whites, and they didn't seem to work out well. Up to that time only three black sisters had been matched with white spouses, and they were

Europeans. Reverend Moon gave me a Canadian, and we were the very first couple to be selected at that matching. As a matter of fact, we were the first interracial Unification couple in America. Reverend Moon said that this is one way that racism could be overcome in America. I'm sure that our relationship can help in some degree to remove the misunderstanding between whites and blacks.

My husband said he had seen me many times while I was in the Performing Arts. He was a complete stranger to me. I had never even seen him before the matching although he had been in the church for twelve years, since he graduated from high school at age seventeen. He was exceptional also in this regard, because the leaders of the church now have made a policy that we would not accept teenagers to full membership. There had been court cases brought against other religious movements, like the International Society for Krishna Consciousness, on the allegation that they abducted and held minor children against their will. The Unification Church has been willing to explain the teachings of Divine Principle to anyone, young or old, but has been careful to recruit only legal adults to full membership. Even though these new members are always responsible adults, fully capable of voluntary commitments to the Unification life of religious service, they have sometimes been kidnapped by parents and deprogrammers.

Even before the Holy Wine ceremony, when my husband and I committed ourselves sacramentally to each other, I wanted God to make the choice for me through his messenger, Reverend Moon. I had long since come to the conclusion that marriage can work well if God is at its beginning and its center. I did not trust myself to make such a momentous decision without divine assistance. I have seen enough divorces among my friends and the effects of broken homes when I worked as resident assistant in the girls' dormitory on the college campus. We both felt that our marriage was not just a private arrangement for our own benefit, but that through marriage and family we might bring about some degree of racial restoration. I really loved this man, form the beginning, and I was resolved to serve him as a very good wife.

After the Holy Wine ceremony we were able to talk for hours about our work in the church and our future together. He was doing a lot of public relations work for the church and had become an important representative in interfaith relations. Our religious backgrounds were similar because he also came from a Catholic family. We both like children and look forward to a nice family, whatever number God wants us to have. We were thrilled to be in the large public wedding in 1982 at the Madison Square Garden, and we both had our parents there. They couldn't understand why we did not leave immediately for a honeymoon. It was a revelation to them that we were willing to postpone our life together for the customary forty days of indemnity, and also for as long as the work of the Church required us to be separated.

The Church teaches that wives should be obedient to their husbands, and that comes out of the Christian tradition as well as from Korean Confucian philosophy, and we think that we should be obedient to God and then to each other. Jesus had a very high regard for women, and Reverend Moon teaches that men and women have the same value to God. They are different expressions of God's creative nature, but they have the same value as sons and daughters of God. In the true love relationship in the church there is no position of either superior or subordinate. True love implies equal harmony. True love is expressed in sacrificial living that goes beyond sex differences. My husband doesn't have a stereotype of me wearing an apron in the kitchen and serving him that way. He understands that very well. When I do things to serve other people he feels that I am also serving him, and he gets inspiration from that.

During the three years between our matching and our marriage my husband continued to work with the brothers and sisters in Washington. The Interfaith Department of the Church has expanded in several directions, some on the level of spiritual and religious programs, some in the areas of theological discussions, and some in working together on community projects. He is very much involved in the social action program of the Washington Council of churches. He is mainly responsible now for a food distribution center, a program that started back in San Francisco when trucks full of surplus vegetables from the Boonville farm were brought into the city. Then the supermarkets and other stores provided large amounts of food that was deemed non-saleable. When the federal government released cheese and other commodities from storage, the members of the Church distributed them to the poor people in the city. My husband has become a first-rate social worker.

Meanwhile, I was enrolled as a student at the Barrytown seminary where college graduates among our members are often invited to attend. This means that the student body of seminarians there are usually in their late twenties, many of them having entered the Church only after graduation from college. The years I spent on the road, touring around with the Performing Arts, were not at all characteristic of life as a dedicated Unificationist. The common perception by observers of our behavior is that we spend most of our time witnessing and fundraising. The fact is that all of us have had those two experiences, but we think of them as implements to do the work of the Church rather than as goals to be achieved. Witnessing to our faith is a means for bringing in new members, and fundraising is a means of sustaining those members. That over-simplifies the distinction between means and ends, but it points to an overriding purpose of the Church's existence.

I am talking here about service to our fellow human beings through the home church program. I had not done this before coming to the seminary, but I am now getting a realistic concept about what Reverend Moon means about the restoration of all creation to God. We say so quickly that in the God-centered family you sacrifice yourself for your spouse and children, the family for the community, the community for the nation, and the nation for the world. Of course, we are here to transform the world, establishing ideal families and an ideal world. When I first joined the Church I thought this restoration would come about in two or three years, and now I've given an extension to say it should happen in my lifetime.

What I am saying is that the daily contact with neighbors in the home church makes one bring these dreams down to reality. We had over fifty seminarians at Barrytown, and in our so-called fieldwork for home church we went out in groups of three instead of singly. Each group focused on one of the churches in the towns up and down the river. The local clergy are used to us now; most of them cooperate, but we also know which ones to avoid. We introduce ourselves as students of ministry and say that "we are studying theology and church history, and we have a lot to learn from you. We just want to come and watch how you do your service, and get to know you, and find out how we can help in your community." Of course, these clergymen have been in their profession for many years, and we know they can teach us a great deal, even while we think we can help them.

It is central to our religious philosophy that we are interdenominational. Unlike a Baptist seminary that can send its students out to practice preaching in their own denominational pulpits, we have no parishes or congregations spotted all over the State. The best we can do is get to sing in the choir of some small church, or even teach a Sunday school class of children. The minister who is glad to get the free help of seminarians in these matters can also point you to individual households where help is needed. This is where the home church concept of human service is applied. You do everything from shovelling snow off their sidewalk to cleaning up their house, putting plastic sheets on the windows to tutoring their children.

There are no hard and fast rules in home church, and practically no limit to the kinds of service you can provide. Home church tries to supply whatever the people need and whatever you are capable of doing. We have many talents among the members. One sister who had nurse's training could care for household elderly people; another knew how to deal with an epileptic youngster. You do all kinds of things. Basically, home church means you are demonstrating Christian love for people by serving them whatever they need, and especially if they cannot get it otherwise. Sometimes they just need you to talk to them, or with failing eyesight they appreciate your reading a magazine to them. We might meet them as a friend and take them to the movies. We go to their church with them. We invite them to come have dinner with us on Sundays.

Home church means you are at home with them, like members of the family. The Kingdom of God, we believe, is the Kingdom of Love, and it goes beyond the boundaries of any given church. The Kingdom of God transcends race and religion and culture. As a youthful Catholic I always believed that all people are the children of God. I thought it was ridiculous to believe that your own church is the one true religion and that God would only love people in that particular church. In the teachings of the Unification Church one of the great attractions is that we are all one in equal value to God and without inequality by sex or race, or age, or position, or religion. We are all God's children, and we just have to learn how we can truly love each other as members of the family.

XII

ANDREW — THE EXPERIENCE OF GOD

In the late summer of 1973 I was standing in the lobby of a London theater waiting for a friend of mine when a short Japanese young lady with a very big smile asked me, "would you buy a magazine for charity?" I asked, "what charity is it?" She said, "we are working to unite all the world's religions." That interested me very much, and I started to read the magazine which was actually criticizing communism. That also interested me, and I said, "why is this about communism if you're talking about uniting world religions?" She couldn't speak English very well. At that point an Englishman came up and started telling me about the Church which he called the Unified Family. He said, "we are teaching a new understanding about God, and we are centrally Christian." So we got into a conversation for over an hour because my friend for whom I was waiting did not turn up.

This was interesting to me because I had been searching for about a year and a half trying to discover how God wanted me to live. That process started me off on a search how I could become a good citizen of the society. I suppose I was a basically religious person, although I was not then going to any church. My mother was Catholic, but my father became disillusioned with the Church for some reason and was then anti-organized religion. I went to Sunday school when I was in primary school, and at the age of twelve I began attending a

Catholic secondary school run by the De Lasalle order of brothers. We had to attend Mass once a week, but most of the students were not at all enthusiastic about that. In those adolescent years I had a real desire to exper- ience God, but the environment of the school was not conducive to a wholehearted devotion to God.

One Sunday, in my local parish I was thinking deeply about the Eucharist. If the Eucharist is the real presence of God, should we not experience something of God's power and His love and His wisdom when we take Communion? As I was coming out of Church I heard some middle-aged women - who had just received the Eucharist - saying bad things about other members of the congregation. This I found incompatible with a belief in the divine presence in the sacrament. The upshot was that I could no longer accept the dogma that the Eucharist is Christ. That so upset my understanding of Catholic teaching that it made me lose faith in Christ- ianity. I didn't lose faith in God. I still believed in God, but I could no longer accept Catholicism.

Maybe I wasn't an exemplary Catholic because I didn't go to the priest or talk to my teachers about such doubts and problems. I was a bit independent in my thoughts, and I made decisions on my own. Even when I was as young as eleven I wanted to have a closer relationship with God and to actually know that he was present in the world. I used to go to confession every week, and I wondered why I couldn't confess directly to God instead of to a priest. I wanted to experience God. From the time I stopped believing in Christianity I concentrated on many different kinds of experiences. When I was at the University I was introduced to

hallucinogenic drugs, especially LSD. After a while I
stopped taking it because it wasn't really helping me to
understand existence. So, when I was twenty-one I left
the University and took a job.

That was when I started reading books, like
Orwell's 1984 and Huxley's Brave New World, but I
couldn't agree with their pessimistic view of the
future. Then someone recommended Huxley's last novel
called Island. In that book he describes a very Utopian
society in the Indian Ocean, combining the art, techno-
logy and science of the West with the spirituality of
the East. The basic spirituality was that of Marijhina
Buddhism which spoke of getting rid of greedy, posses-
sive selfhood. So I reflected on my own life style and
admitted that I was living a selfish life. I began to
read simple handbooks about Zen Buddhism and Yoga, and
especially the Teachings of Don Juan, and another book
called The Center of the Cyclone. These books made the
point that drugs helped you to have a religious experience only if you took them with the intention of having
such an experience.

This seemed reasonable enough, and the first time I
took LSD with the purpose of having a religious
experience I felt a tremendous widening of my mind. I
was looking at objects that were metal or plastic or
glass, but internally to me there was a common essence
which was God. Then another time, again on LSD, I felt
that everything in my room was accusing me of being
unworthy and sinful. I was determined to overcome that
feeling by concentrating all my senses. But, as the
hallucinations continued I felt I was very dirty, that I
had to wash myself all over. I concentrated all my

senses - touch, sight, taste, smell, and hearing - and I
began to hear music where there wasn't any music.

At that point there began a kind of flashing white
light, keeping in time with my heartbeat. I was
reminded of something in the Teaching of Don Juan which
was quite similar. It was the belief that the power
contained in peyote was the incarnation of Mescalito. I
thought that my spirit would be taken out of my body,
and I was a bit afraid. Then I decided that I should be
willing to let that happen, and that I would rather be
with God than to stay here on earth. Through that
experience I realized that life was very sacred and that
everything man can do is something very precious. All
forms of human art are actually celebrations of each of
the abilities God has given us. We can celebrate our
divine abilities to do art, to draw lines, to write
symphonies, to make music.

The genuine personal experience of God continued to
elude me. I took up some books about the North American
Red Indian religion. They kept looking for the right
road; they would go to a mountain top and cry for a
vision to tell them how to lead their lives. I was sure
that God did exist and that somehow he could guide us.
Just about a month before I met the Japanese woman in
front of the theater someone recommended that I read
Yoganada's Autobiography of a Yogi. He was the revered
founder of the Self-Realization Fellowship and taught
that the doctrines of Jesus were in complete harmony with
those of Bhagavan Krishna. In that book he spoke about
the Bible. His guru gave an explanation of the Fall of
Man as a sexual sin. He said also that the Hindus
venerated Jesus as one of the incarnations of God. When

I left the Catholic Church I had read Nietzsche's <u>Anti-Christ</u> and had become very negative about Christianity. So this was like making me again open-minded toward Jesus, with the notion that he could have been like an Indian Holy Man who worked miracles.

That was definitely a kind of preparation for meeting that Japanese Unificationist woman. So, when they told me their religion was centrally Christian I was willing to listen to them. They invited me to their center in South London, and two weeks later when I had a free Saturday, I went down and heard the first lecture on the Principle of Creation. There were only a few people there, the Japanese lady and the brother I had first met; there was one Italian lady and two other British men. This was their living quarters where they gave lectures on the <u>Divine</u> <u>Principle</u>. They were also actively fundraising so that they could send members to America for more education and training. In the evenings they would go out and sell those anit-communist magazines; they also sold candles and asked for dona-tions.

At first I went to the London center about once a week, and later on more often. So, over a period of about eight weeks I heard all the lectures on the <u>Divine</u> <u>Principle</u>. The last few chapters of the book I heard at the British headquarters, a large farmhouse in the country west of London where they also held workshops. In listening to the <u>Principle</u> I got a better understand-ing about God. I was reintroduced to the God of the Bible, how the Father loves His children. I developed a personal relationship with God, understood the mission of Jesus and why He was crucified. I was especially impressed with the parallel periods of history, and how God had been working to bring the Messiah again. Some parts of the Principle remained questionable to me, but I think I accepted about eighty percent of it.

The important thing is that my heart was moved, and I was developing a personal relationship with God. This teaching showed me that I must live my life for God, even though it may not be the complete truth. I was recommended to do some sort of indemnity condition. So that's what I did. On the Monday, Tuesday and Wednesday after the workshop weekend I did a three-day fast. I re-read the parts of the Principle that I wasn't sure about. I didn't get any revelations or any personal spiritual experiences, but I just somehow felt confirmed in the things I had accepted. I felt it was right for me to dedicate my life to God. I recalled that I had read the biography of Saint Francis Xavier when I was about thirteen, and had been excited that he dedicated himself to the evangelization of the East. I began to renew myself with prayer, to feel the heart of God about which the Principle was telling me, a God of grief and sorrow, hurt by the sins of man but longing for an ideal.

The following week, about eight days after the workshop, I gave notice to my employer. He was surprised because I had only just previously been asking for more money. He said, "oh, we'll give you a raise," but I told him that I was not interested any more. I told my landlord that I was moving out, and it was all right with him. One problem I had was that I owed a hundred pounds to a friend and didn't know how I could pay him. When I told him about my religious conversion he forgave me the debt. So the process of joining the Church was very simple. I can't even remember whether I signed an application or a membership card. There was no formal procedure. I simply moved into the community that was situated just outside of Reading, north of London. I worked in our publishing outlet there, especially on our anti-communist newspaper called The Rising Tide.

After three months of that I did a year and a half of basic membership tasks, fundraising and witnessing all over, in Scotland and Wales, North Ireland and England itself. It was teamwork, sometimes with two or three members, sometimes as many as eight. Then an international witnessing team was formed, and we moved to Germany in the autumn of 1975. This was called the first global IOWC team (International One World Crusade). For three months we cooperated with CARP on the campus of the University of Frankfurt. We held the usual lectures on Unification theory and distributed pamphlets, and sometimes had conflict with communist students. It was even worse when we went to France for several months where students came up to us on the street and physically prevented us from witnessing. The big problem in France was that many Catholic youth groups were working hand-in-hand with the communist youth and causing conflict with us on the city streets.

In 1976 the second global team of the International One-World Crusade was composed of about 120 members from twenty-seven countries and sent on a mission to Japan. Each Westerner worked with a Japanese partner, and we asked people to answer a questionnaire. If they were interested in religion we would invite them to our center for a meal or a lecture. The Unification Church was then a fast-growing religion in Japan, especially on the university campus. The CARP movement was concentrating on anti-communist activity. Our Japanese members were successful in the ideological dialogue with communists, so that their leaders ordered them not to debate the Unificationists. At the end of 1977 the whole team moved to Korea where we gained further education about the origin and growth of our Church.

After a few months of education and witnessing in Korea the global team was dispersed, with the members going back to get involved again in their own country's activities. I returned to London, worked with the publishing group for almost six months and also did a fair share of witnessing. In May, 1978, I was happily matched by Reverend Moon with a German sister who is also a designer and artist, doing the same kind of work in the mission of publishing. We knew that we would be separated until Reverend Moon announced the next formal mass wedding ceremony. In a peripheral sense then I cooperated with the graduates of the Barrytown seminary when they came to Britain in the summer of 1978 to institute the home church program. When they left I welcomed the invitation to return to Korea, the Church homeland, for which I had developed much affection. I stayed there three years as a trainee in the Supradenominational Christian Association, an ecumenical group with the purpose of getting Christians of all denominations to cooperate for the common good. This was not a Unificationist project, but it received financial support from the Church. It was started in 1966 by a group of Christian leaders, one of whom was a Unification Church member. There was no Catholic priest among the founders, but we really got more cooperation - or less opposition - from the Catholics than from some of the fundamentalist Protestant preachers who forbade their members to talk with us.

The purpose of the Association was to reconcile the antagonisms among the Christian denominations rather than to gain members for the Unification Church. Each denomination has its own seminary, and we tried to contact theologians and professors for discussions about our similarities and our differences. Their cooperation was reluctant because their church officials were publicly opposed not only to our religion but also to each other. One prominent minister was expelled from his denomination when he accepted the presidency of the Association. Reverend Moon had faith in this ecumenical movement. That's why he selected the five of us from different countries, Britain, France, Germany, Italy, and Spain, so that we could bring the program to our native lands.

Back in Britain we were married in 1981, but then we both returned to Korea to share the same mission of publication, writing and editing. We learned a great deal about Korea where the Church continues to suffer some disabilities. For example, President Pak had some Christians among his advisors who opposed the Church. The same is true of President Chun Doo Hwan, whose wife is a Christian and not favorably disposed to our Church. Our foundation bought land for an international university, but many high level ministers of the Protestant Churches blocked our plans to build, and we could not get permission to build. We applied for permission also to build a Unification seminary, and even though the government allows each denomination to establish its own seminary they still haven't granted us permission to build. In America the Church complains that the Barrytown seminary has not been accredited to grant academic degrees, but at least the seminary exists and functions successfully.

My wife and I stayed in Seoul to continue in the Ecumenical Association but also to work with Dr. Sang Hun Lee in the Unification Thought Institute which he established for the education of staff members of the Church. This is a presentation of the Unification Principle as a philosophical system, comparing it with traditional thought systems. Then we also helped out with the Professors, World Peace Academy. We designed and produced an English language brochure for them. We also transcribed the many tapes from the proceedings of the 1981 International Conference on the Unity of Sciences. We then asked permission to return to England, and arrived there for Christmas, 1982.

It was my vague intention to return to the university to study for an academic degree, but when I got back to London I found that in the aftermath of the Daily Mail libel case the Church hadn't made as much progress as I had expected. In fact, we had suffered considerably from that publicity and from the adverse court judgment. I looked to find where I could be of most use and was asked to fill a vacancy in the publications department. For about eight months then I did this kind of work, editing a magazine and overseeing other publications. Then I was invited to cooperate with the Ecumenical Research Association, the New ERA, and the ecumenical enterprises.

We make sacrifices to carry on the work of the Church while we are still unmarried, and we have learned to anticipate that these sacrifices will continue during our married life. In the marriage of two Unificationists there is an enormous amount of mutual support that is spiritual and social, psychological and physical. In spite of our celibate and prayerful preparation for marriage we are still confronted with our fallen nature and our bad habits. The problems are in a minor key, that is, the small day-by-day aspects of human relations between my wife and me. I think she struggles a bit with the kind of concerns that are logical for women to face. Obviously she thinks, perhaps more than I do, about settling down, about keeping the home, about our material security.

We both recognize, of course, that the Unification life style is quite different from the lifestyle that most people have, like staying in one place, remaining together and doing a job that becomes a career. My wife has gone on the 40-day mission of witnessing even after our two children were born. The children are looked after in our nursery, and we understand the need to make spiritual conditions. The whole teaching of Reverend Moon is to sacrifice self for family, family for the nation, and nation for the world. Reverend Moon has said that the ideology of Jesus was that the life of sacrifice is very necessary if we want to restore the world to God. We can't be true to the teachings of Divine Principle if we don't practice them in everyday life. Reverend Moon is living this way himself; he is showing us the way.

My wife and I were privileged to be with Reverend Moon when he spoke with the members in Korea. When we were in training for ecumenical mission we went with him to Lake Chung Chou, where there is a training center. We prayed together and talked together. We went with him walking in the fields and up the hills. I see him as the person who is successor to the earthly tasks of Jesus. We believe that Jesus met with him when he was sixteen years old and asked him to take on the mission of building the Kingdom of Heaven on earth. I see him as a man of incredible determination, someone who has struggled against tremendous odds, but has always kept the vision of solving the problems of sin and evil, planning practical activities that can restore God's sovereignty on the earth. I really believe that he is closely cooperating with Jesus. He carries the unfulfilled heart of Jesus. I don't conceive of him as divine, but he is a supreme example of a man who has total self-mastery.

Sometimes there is a temptation to be impatient at the slow progress we are making in the Moonie program for universal restoration. The world is not changing as fast as I thought it would when I first learned God's plan as outlined in <u>Divine Principle</u>. I am not discouraged because I know enough of history to realize that important changes do not happen quickly. Yet, I often feel sad for so many persons who don't respond fast enough to the invitation that God extends to them.

XIII

PATRICIA — THE CONTINUING CATHOLIC

My younger brother preceded me into the Church, but he never pressured me to join with him. His occasional letters to me were unexpectedly spiritual for a man who had never been particularly religious when he was at home. I was happy because in his letters I saw that he was doing something that made him happy. He joined the church in Colorado, and my parents were upset because he wasn't going on to medical school. My mother would sit and cry, "Oh, my son has left the Catholic Church." I told her, "You know he wasn't exactly doing so well as a Catholic. You know he was searching and wasn't sure about many things."

Perhaps we could call ourselves a typical Catholic family. I was raised with seven brothers and one sister, and my parents were both loving and sacrificial. We were a family of high moral and religious traditions. We often prayed the Rosary together on our knees. We sat in one of the front pews at Sunday Mass, and my parents were active leaders in our home parish. I played the organ in church and sang in the choir. I was active in the Sodality. I went to parochial and Catholic schools all my life. I went to college at the Jesuit Creighton University in Omaha, and spent my junior year abroad at the Sorbonne.

People ask me how I got converted to the Unification Church, but I have to say that I did not have a religious conversion. I was always curious about God, and that began when I was a very young girl. I wanted to become a nun, up until I was in high school. I asked questions about the nature of God, the meaning of three persons in one God. Another major question was the problem of evil. If there is a good God who is absolute, how could He have created evil? Many times my professors said that "certain things we have to accept on faith alone. Don't ask any further. This is your personal responsibility to believe in your faith."

My search for truth continued in Paris where I spent my junior college year and studied existentialism. I became very dissatisfied and very lonely because there wasn't any spiritual fire in France. I talked with some of the priests in different parishes after Sunday Mass, and asked why the Churches were empty. After all, France is a Catholic country. One priest said, "they just quit. Perhaps less than five percent of the people in France go to church on Sundays." That was just after the Vatican council closed, when I was twenty years old. Many people think that the changes introduced by the Council raised doubts about the Church and caused a drop-off in Mass attendance. I don't think I was influenced by those changes.

My main study interests in college were philosophy and theology, and I graduated with a liberal arts degree. Then I got a position with the Fidelity Mutual Insurance Company, and I soon became a successful insurance underwriter. Three years after college I met and married another successful insurance broker. He had been born and raised in England. He was a kind and loving person, but had no interest in any religion or church. We moved to California where our son was born. Our family life became more problematic as I kept searching for more satisfactory spiritual experiences. I continued in the formal practice of the Catholic religion, praying, going to Mass and receiving the sacraments regularly. When we moved back to Omaha we both continued making good money in the insurance business. Nevertheless, I began to feel that the more I sought spiritual answers the shakier our marriage became.

My search led me to the Divine Light Mission, in my hometown of Omaha, where several of my friends were absorbed in the study of the Hindu religion. I was very much interested in the way they were living and the manner in which they combined personal prayer and service to others. They did not just center on the commune and exclude the rest of the world. I became thoroughly involved with this spiritual community where God told me one thing very strongly, even though I had heard it often before. He said that the whole purpose of life is to serve others. It was at that point, even before I heard about the Divine Principle, that I quit my job, closed out my bank account, gave away my clothes. I was cooking food for hungry people, helping the poor as much as I could, trying to learn how to please God by being of service to others.

My brother was then at the Unification center in Boulder, Colorado, and he phoned to say that he and the regional director wanted to stop at our home in Omaha on their way to the Madison Square Rally in September, 1975. They came as our guests and had dinner with us. That night they spent two hours in an overview of the

Divine Principle. Before they left the next morning
they told me more about their teachings and gave me a
copy of the book. I studied it pretty carefully for one
month, while I kept going for meditation at my spiritual
community of the Divine Light Mission. I was also
praying and reading the Bible, and going to the Catholic
Church on Sundays.

During that month I really tried to make sense of
the Unification Church. I wrote down twenty-five
questions I had, about the content of the Divine
Principle, and got a phone call from New York giving
answers to all of them. At that time there wasn't much
negative publicity about Reverend Moon, and I had no
fixed preconceptions about his Church. Like my mother I
had real doubts about the Moonies, so she and I went
over to Creighton to talk with the Jesuit priests there.
They didn't seem to know much at all about the movement,
and gave the impression that my parents weren't raising
us right if we were getting involved in such strange
religion. They said, "why don't you just check it out
and come to your own conclusions." I said I might do
that, and I told my mother I'd go to Boulder and check
out her wayward son.

I decided first to go to Denver for two weeks to
look further into the Divine Light Mission there and to
study and pray some at their big ashram. I was already
twenty-eight years old and still searching for religious
knowledge and spiritual peace. If I was going through a
conversion experience it certainly wasn't something
sudden like Saint Paul's. From Denver I called up my
brother in Boulder, went there and had lunch with him.
He invited me to a lecture that night and arranged for

me to stay over at the Boulder Center. I had a long talk with one of their members, a medical doctor who was working in spiritual therapy. I spent three days at the center, listening to lectures on the <u>Divine</u> <u>Principle</u> and talking with members. The main lecturer was a man who had been in Africa doing missionary work for the Unification Church, and he really inspired me.

What happened there was that I really found God. Inside my heart God came to me as a real person, the God who created all things, who existed always, God the father, God the eternal, God the absolute. What I then realized was that God has a heart just like me, that he has feelings just like me. I had a deep experience of discovery that really happened to me. Of course, God knew that I had been looking for him all my life. I had my ups and downs. I had lived in other countries. I had been lonely and often felt forsaken. Through the <u>Divine</u> <u>Principle</u> I now understood the Trinity. That was important for me to come to understand the source of all life. I understood God to be my father and my mother, that God was suffering, and that when I sin He suffers more.

The insight that God is a God of heart was new to me. Before that I saw that God was transcendent and at a distance from me. In other words, when I sinned, maybe I was hurting myself, but I didn't understand how my sin could offend God, hurt His heart. It is as if you walk away from me when I tell you I love you. Sin is like saying to God, "I hate you; I don't want any-thing to do with you." Now my relationship with God was so close that I knew my sins made Him suffer. This became my awareness, and it came completely. This was happening in my heart, and all of a sudden I understood that God was suffering.

When I heard people praying at the center I was very moved. Instead of a Hail Mary they were praying "Dear Heavenly Father." I went into this room all by myself and made a vow. I said, "Heavenly Father, I'm really sorry I hurt You all my life. I'm sorry that You're suffering, and I want You to know that I will help You. I feel You need me. I will dedicate my life so that people will know how beautiful You are, and I'll try never to hurt You again. I want You to know one thing: I"ll never leave You." So this was my vow. To me it was equivalent to what a nun vows to God. No human told me to do it. It was from my own heart, out of love for God. I've stayed faithful to that vow when my family and my friends, and even people I didn't know, ridiculed me and mocked me, and tried to make me change.

After all my wandering, spiritually, philosophically, I now found my permanent home when I was almost twenty-nine years old. In one way, it was time to settle down. I'd had several good professional jobs, lived in other countries. I had seen a lot of life and was now about to lose my husband and son. He refused to convert to the Unification Church, and I soon learned that Reverend Moon's blessing for marriage could not be given to only one spouse in the couple. We had separated on several occasions, and my attachment to the Unification Church spelled permanent estrangement between us. It was no sacrifice for me to release him, but he insisted on taking our son to England.

Meanwhile, I did not go back to Omaha but lived at the Boulder center where my brother was, and I appreciated that we could give each other good support. I spent two years there, mainly in fundraising but also in absorbing more of the Divine Principle by prayer, reading and discussion. I really learned the Moonie way of life with other dedicated members of the Church. Moonies do a lot of travelling around the country, and we had frequent visits from groups who came through as mobile fundraising teams, and also on the International One World Crusade.

My next mission was on the West Coast, witnessing for the most part to students at Berkeley, California. Reverend Moon made a special plea that we gain members to build up his task forces in America. I worked hard and for long hours trying to reach people on the streets and on the campus. I was out on that campus every day. I fasted. I did conditions. I prayed, and I was able to attract fifteen spiritual children in one year. These are the people who stayed on to become members, out of the large numbers of prospects who came to the house for a meal and a lecture. Even when they come for a weekend workshop we win relatively few members from among them, perhaps one out of eight or ten. This belies the slander among our enemies who fear the enormous seductive powers of persuasion that Moonies are supposed to have. Of course, we need dedicated members to carry on the large organizational work of the Church, all its programs and plans, but we work in the service of all mankind.

This is why I don't think it's correct to say that we shift our religious affiliation when we join the

Unification Church. We continue to represent the Church we used to attend but with a different emphasis and more accurate destination. For example, I have looked for the good in the Catholic church, and I embrace it. I actually feel more strongly Catholic than I ever did in my life, and the reason is simple. I feel more the universality of Catholicism and what that really means when I say the Apostles' Creed. I feel that God is working everywhere through all religions, and I want to work together with people of all religions. I don't consider myself separate, or in another denomination. Our concept of unification supersedes all sectarian boundaries. I feel that God is working through us and is calling all people of all religious faiths to come together in His name at this time.

Everyone knows that the movement and its founder have met animosity from many people who profess to be faithful Christians. My parents were angry when my brother joined the Church, and when I joined it was even more frustrating to them, so they never really accepted it. One family member reacted in an interesting fashion. Mike was always the model son and brother. He served in the Navy for eight years, and when he came out he entered the seminary to study for the diocesan priesthood. I think a little bit of it was his reaction to Tom and me being in the Unification Church, and to my parents' grief about not having a priest in the family. He has not communicated much with me, but on one occasion he almost came to see me at the Barrytown seminary. He phoned to say that he was on his way, but then I am sure my mother persuaded him not to come. This continues to be a problem, that my parents are a stumbling block between me and my brothers and sisters.

Perhaps my family is representative of middle-class parents who sacrificed a great deal for their children, gave us a good moral example, sent us through good Catholic schools, provided the environment in which to develop a close relationship with God. What happened to us? My older brother, Jerry, came back from Viet Nam a decorated hero but a very changed and rebellious person who has gone his own wayward path, clearly not a member of any church. My brother John has lost all interest in religion, at least in the organized church. My only sister, Rochelle, is a Montessori teacher doing an excellent job with children but doesn't go to Mass any more. I was not able to get back to Omaha for her wedding last year. My two youngest brothers, Joe and Tim, are both at Creighton University, but I heard that Tim is involved in drugs. It's just wild what's happening in my family, and all I can guess is that they are struggling and searching.

A lot of the Moonies used to be Catholic, and most of them continue to love and respect the Church, but they don't get respect and love in return. I think that's unwise. I have gone back to the Catholic church to offer my services, but they rejected me because I am a Moonie. For example, when I was at the seminary a group of us volunteered to work for Father Bruce Ritter down in New York City where he is helping kids who are caught up in sex exploitation. We phoned and said we are students at the Unification Theological Seminary, and offered to do volunteer work with them. The manager said that because the seminary isn't accredited they wouldn't take our help.

Another experience of mine had personal overtones. I had met a wonderful Franciscan sister who invited me to stay at her convent in Newark while I was fundraising there for a short time. Later in the year I called her and said, "I have two and a half weeks between semesters, and I want to do some volunteer work with you. What can I do to help you out?" She said that I wasn't needed there. Sister Mary Anne had been pressured by the other nuns, or by her superior, not to have anything to do with Moonies. When I first visited there they did not know I was a Moonie and they loved me in a genuine Christian love, but now I was ostracized. I simply switched my fieldwork to a nondenominational group of blacks in Harlem. Three of our seminary students had worked with them before, and they are always glad to have our help. I didn't even have to go down to the city for an interview.

My seminary experience is something worth talking about. I had been in the Church only two years when I was accepted as a student at Barrytown. The seminary opened in 1975, and I was in the third class to enter in 1977. I suppose my academic record at Creighton University, and the fact that I was already thirty-one years old, were partial reasons for sending me to the seminary. I took the prescribed series of courses, prayed and played with my sisters and brothers there, but I concentrated my best efforts on a study of the Catholic church. I did a forty-five page report on the Society of Jesus. I admire the sacrifices of the saints and martyrs of the Church, and I think that God has reached enormous numbers of people in the world because of the heroic work of great, great people in the Catholic Church. I continue to study the history of the

Church, and I know the fluctuations of morality in the Vatican as well as the saintly lives of great intellectuals and great missionaries. It is my Catholic background, I'm sure, that attracts me to a more thorough knowledge of the Church, and I would say that I am probably more Catholic now than I ever was.

I was matched by Reverend Moon in 1979 after finishing my studies at the seminary. Often we do not know the person with whom we are matched, or have only a passing acquaintance with our future spouse. In my case I did have at least some contact with the man who is now my husband. Out in Southern California, where I fundraised and did public relations for the movement for more than three years, he lived in the same center, but we just barely knew each other. It so happened that we were both in the same class at the seminary where the brothers and sisters tend to associate at various levels in the pursuit of knowledge. In our practice and principle concerning celibacy we train ourselves to think of our classmates as members of the family and not as future marriage partners. We had no idea that we would be matched.

We have told each other many times that Reverend Moon's choice came as a real surprise. We had never thought of each other, or of anybody else as a specific prospective mate. This fact is probably hard for a nonmember of the Church to believe. We have to keep our hearts open to fulfill the will of God. When I was there with all the other sisters and brothers who had been invited to the matching ceremony I was really trying to keep a faithful heart to trust in God and to allow him to work through Reverend Moon. I began to notice during the process that the couples Reverend Moon brought together looked as though they were sister and brother. Here I was in this room with a thousand brothers and I looked around and prayed, "Heavenly Father, who in this room looks like one of my brothers?" I saw Neil across the room, and I said, "if anyone here looks like my brother, he does." I put this right out of my mind as an inappropriate thought, but the next morning I was matched to him.

It was a three-year wait until the mass wedding at Madison Square Garden in July, 1982, and we hardly ever saw each other in all that time. He continued to do paralegal work for the Church on the East Coast, and my time was spent mainly in southern California where I was engaged mainly in public relations. Since I was already thirty-six years old at the time of the wedding, and was most anxious to have children, we had only the forty-day delay before we finally began to live together. Reverend Moon is ready to make exceptions for the members who marry in their thirties.

XIV

EDWARD — RIGORS OF CONVERSION

Until the time I left home, at age seventeen, I went through the typical Protestant routine of going to Church and even going through the whole Sunday school program. My mother was a very strong Presbyterian, but my father was anti-religion, and I adopted his stance basically. I never joined the Church, and I rejected institutional Christianity, but I knew there was something special about Jesus. I didn't repudiate spirituality and the ideals of religion, but I just saw that these were not being practiced in the Christianity to which I was exposed. Occasionally I would go back to a church, Presbyterian or otherwise, just to check it out again, but I'd always come away disillusioned.

California is the place to find varieties of religion. I attended the University at Davis, and got myself a bachelor's degree in mathematics. Some of my good friends were "Jesus Freaks," or were in the Jesus movement, at Berkeley. I was very much impressed with something in them, their spirituality, but what disillusioned me with them was their mindlessness. I saw no intellectual substance to it. I went over to their house for dinner at Resurrection City. They burned the beans and somebody said, "Oh, praise the Lord." It just wasn't for real, although I think they were sincere in their love for God. I have to admit it was a little tiresome to hear them chant "Praise the Lord."

Then I had contact with several other religious movements. I like the Meher-Baba group a lot and was interested in different yoga communes that do transcendental meditation. In fact, I practiced yoga for a while on my own. I was also involved with drugs, but in my point of view at the time it was not always integrated with spiritual search. Sometimes it was just an intoxication. Experiences with psychedelic drugs did lead me to the realization that the higher levels of consciousness have a value far out of proportion with career success, or making money, or anything worldly, so to speak. I didn't cast these experiences in terms of institutional religion, but I did sometimes feel religious quite aside from churches. It wasn't a Protestant thing. It was to attain a certain level of spirit, of communion with God, or with the One, or with whatever you want to call it.

Music was my favorite pastime. While I was still in college I formed a band that made loud rock music, and made some money when any organization was willing to hire us. I had a beard and long hair, and I dressed like the other weirdos on campus. After graduation I kept the band going, and I acted pretty much like the hippies, but I had my own apartment and didn't live in a commune. I had gotten to the point in my life when I thought maybe the only way to find happiness was to get married. One day I was sitting there looking out of the window, meditating about nothing, when I heard a voice in my mind saying: "If you go out right now, the first girl you meet is the one you will marry."

The first girl I met then was a bright and happy person standing in the shopping center selling sandwiches. This was in North Oakland near the College of Arts and Crafts. She turned out to be a Unification member, and was naturally very open to having people walk up and talk with her. We had a great conversation, and she invited me over to the center. At first I viewed her as a potential mate in a romantic way, but after a couple visits to the house I realized that that was not appropriate because she was a sister to me. She was very pure. She loved me, but there was no sense of romance or of exclusive possessiveness. She was concerned about me and looked after me. I was so impressed with her because that just was not the way other people operated.

About two weeks later I heard my first introductory lecture on the general notions about God's relation to the world. It was presented by Dr. Durst, who is now American president of the Church. We then had a very stimulating discussion with a brother, David Store, who was willing to go into some of the intellectual questions I had. The lectures on Wednesday nights were basically for new people, but after several weeks I started going on other nights to listen to the more advanced lectures about the teachings of the Divine Principle. The idea of moving in permanently came from a friend of mine who knew I was dissatisfied with my apartment and that my lease would run out on February first. I told him about this group I had met, and he said, "why don't you move in with the family?" I talked to Christina who was assistant to Onni Durst, the director of the center. She said it would be possible, but "of course, if you move in you'll have to give up your band."

This was a serious moment of my life, and maybe God was protecting me. I was beginning to see that moving in with the Moonies represented a totally, radically different alternative life style. It was either or, the music scene or the family, and I was definitely now ready to give up the former for the latter. I had my rent paid up to the end of January, and Christina, my spiritual mother, said, "please move in as soon as you can, the sooner the better." The closer I got to the end of January the more urgent I felt the need to move. It was like the Jesus people told me: "You take one step toward Jesus. He takes two steps toward you." When I did move in I felt like there was a huge door slamming behind me. It seemed to me I had gotten in just at the last possible second. If I had waited another day, something would have prevented me. One other incident might shed light on this attitude. Several days after I moved in I heard the first official Divine Principle lecture, which was given by one of the older sisters. After the lecture someone asked: "Is Reverend Moon the Messiah?" She just very calmly said, "Yes." Nobody followed it up, but I felt my spirit in shock. I was astonished.

Something happened to me that is hard to describe. Consciously I just took it in, but I think my ancestors were there to support me. I said to myself, "I can't handle this right now - this idea of the Messiah living now on earth." All these connotations about Jesus probably flooded in from my ancestors. It was too much for me, and I said "I'm just going to shelve this for six months, or even longer," and I did. I stopped thinking about Messiahship and what it would mean in my own life. Basically I was sure that the movement was good. Whatever else was going on, I found that these people were incredibly good. So, how things were labeled was secondary to me. Just because the sister made that claim didn't dissuade me or change my opinion.

In the first week or so, when I lived in the community, I had a lot of spiritual experiences. I guess that within maybe even the first few days I knew that this was really for me. I realized that I had to stay, that this was the place for me, but also that there were great forces at work to make people leave. As it turns out, I met someone who left just shortly after I moved in. He was coming back for his luggage, and he said, "Oh, this family is real nice, but you would leave after a while." From that point, for at least seven or eight months, I was afraid that I would leave. I set up a fortress in myself against the evil forces, and I was determined that I would not leave. For quite a while I was really struggling.

There was no formal entrance ceremony. There is a form of acceptance, and I think I signed a year or two later. It says something like "I accept the basic teachings of the <u>Divine</u> <u>Principle</u>," but there was nothing in it concerning Reverend Moon. Even before I moved in I felt very accepted by everyone. You're a brother, and you have the feeling that you are coming home. I felt that even when I just came over to visit. Another significant moment was the recitation of the Unification pledge. In the Oakland group the younger members do not say the pledge, and I said it two months after moving in. The concluding words of the pledge are: "I will fight with my life. I will be responsible for accomplishing my duty and mission. This I pledge and swear." I felt that taking the pledge for the first time was like a solemn initiation.

At the time I moved in, in 1973, it was just when our fundraising activities, for which we are famous, were getting off the ground. The first MFT's, mobile fundraising teams, were organized that spring, but didn't really get institutionalized until the fall of 1973. One of the members of my team was Barbara Underwood, who was really on fire for the Lord. She and Steve Hasson were ten times as zealous as I was, just really zapped out with intense fervor. Several other people I know, who are now active opponents to the Church, were unusual in their fervent zeal for the Church. I think that the external activity has to have a deep internal and spiritual commitment to God. You need that strength to fight against Satan and to ward off his temptations. These defectors never really came to a mature understanding of what they were doing. When they were confronted by the deprogrammers they got swept away. They also had a lot of resentment about how much work they had done for the Church.

The so-called deprogrammers are hired by parents who are willing to pay the high cost of abducting their daughter or son from a religious movement. My own parents lived about two hundred miles from the Bay area when they came to visit me. They came to the center to pick me up. I had a truck-driving job at the time, and they were waiting for me when I came in wearing overalls. But I had short hair and no beard. I looked clean and respectable, as compared to the last time I saw them, two years previously. I think they were pleased and surprised by the improvement. They talked with some of the members and said they were completely uplifted by this Church and by these people.

One of the reasons my parents came was that we were slated to attend the annual stockholders' meeting of an investment company in which my father had invested, and in which I had about five thousand dollars in stocks. That very night, at the meeting, I told him that I was going to cash in my investment and give it to the movement. I was twenty-four at the time, and they saw no reason to dissuade me. My father, who was pretty cynical about organized religion, always complained that churchgoers are not real true Christians. He would say, "Christianity would be great if it were put into practice." After he talked with the members at the center he said, "These people are true Christians." That's a precious testimony to my spiritual commitment, and I'll never forget it.

That was the last time I saw my parents for about two and a half years. During that time they attended several parents' workshops conducted by the Unification Church. They are not completely sold on what I am doing, but they are in no way negative. They just feel that I am old enough to know what I am doing, and that for me it is basically good. Right now, they think I am too dependent on the church. In their minds - especially my father's - they thought this was a phase I was passing through, and that after a few years I would grow out of it and get a regular job. I'm not doing that, and I don't intend to. They will have to recognize that I am a permanent part of the church. It's probably similar to the relationship between Catholic parents and their son going to the seminary.

After a few months I was asked if I wanted to become a missionary and go down to Los Angeles, but I felt that I wasn't ready, and there was no pressure on me. Later on I accepted the invitation to be a missionary and go further away. This time I did feel ready to attempt it, even though I didn't know where I was to go. I ended up going to Durham, New Hampshire, where we had a very small center near the University. There we witnessed among the students and did fundraising only one day a week, just to support the center. This was our central location in the State where we gradually built up enough membership that we decided to open a satellite center in Manchester. Two of us went there to pioneer, rented a small apartment and witnessed for new members, but it folded after two months for lack of members.

My next assignment, at the end of the year, was New York City, where I encountered Japanese members for the first time. Reverend Moon was sending in a lot of Japanese to give muscle to the American family. I had had an interest in Japan even before I joined the family, because I was very much into Zen. I loved those Japanese because they taught me so much, and it was through them that I had a kind of second rebirth of spirituality. They are really Calvinistic and are very repentant of sins. God is everything to them, and they are completely obedient to the will of God. It seems to me that there is an affinity here with the Jesuits since

Calvin and Loyola were in the same place, the University of Paris, at the same time.

Meanwhile, the Church was able to purchase the New Yorker Hotel, which was converted into our World Mission Center. This became our most important educational center, especially for members who were called in periodically for refresher courses of workshops and seminars. It was actually by being on the staff there that I was able to get a full appreciation of the complete <u>Divine</u> <u>Principle</u>. The best lecturer there was Wayne Miller, and it was through him that I not only got the whole picture of our Church teaching but also a methodology for teaching. You have to study and learn, but it is by preparing and giving lectures that you learn even better. At this point I also did public relations work for the Madison Square campaign in 1975.

After two years in New York, spent almost exclusively on workshops, seminars and retreats, my spiritual life was getting sort of stale. I was willing to take more responsibility, but to do that I needed a stronger, deeper spiritual base, which somehow was not developing in the routine I was following. I needed something new and more difficult, where I could pay indemnity to God. So I volunteered for a mobile fundraising team because it's the most difficult way to serve the Church. It's also the most enriching experience, an activity in which you really confront yourself and God and Satan. This is complete self-sacrifice, where you practice a great deal of humility, obedience and perseverance. In my own experience in MFT centers, I have not seen anything that is more demanding and more rigorous. You go everywhere; you face bigotry and antagonism, and you get an education that can't be communicated. I wonder whether the early Franciscan mendicants had such a tough time in medieval Europe.

The Barrytown seminary opened in 1975. I didn't have any great desire to go there, but my central figure said that everybody had to fill out an application form. It wasn't till the following year, just before the Washington Monument Rally, I got notification that I had been accepted to the seminary. It was a real surprise to me, but I was excited about it. I then went through the typical experience of a lot of the members who go to Barrytown: The need to readjust from the hectic front-line hard work, every-minute-is-God's-minute existence, which has a work-ethic aspect, to the seminary where you live a student's life. For the first couple of weeks I felt almost guilty; I felt accused by the spirit world for not working hard, for sleeping six hours a night. Obviously we have to have a balance of grace and works. The seminary was good for me because it provided something broader than constant external activity as a way to heaven.

The members who go to the seminary have already finished college, but most of them had majored in the sciences with a few English majors and one or two philosophy majors among the women. I had never taken a college course in religion as an undergraduate, and I think this was true of ninety percent of the Barrytown seminarians. The seminary courses we had in the first year had to be introductory and very general, like a survey of comparative religions, Church history starting with Patristics, and broad interpretations of both the Old and the New Testaments. It wasn't till my second year - which was the third year of the seminary's existence - that we had a course developed in Unification theology by Young Oon Kim. She taught a course also on Unification polity which was very difficult, because our polity was so diffuse.

We didn't have summer school at the seminary, so after the first year it was MFT again. After graduation in 1978 we had the big push for home church experience in England. That was great, because during those two years in the seminary I often wondered whether I was really growing. It wasn't till I got back in the field and assumed a leadership position that I realized how much the seminary experience had helped me to grow. For the first time I thoroughly enjoyed this type of work and felt most comfortable in dealing with people from all over Europe. Our main focus was home church in Scotland as well as England.

We didn't hear anything about home church, at least in America, before 1978, but I think that functionally it was the same thing they had been doing all along in Korea. For legal and social reasons the Church in Korea did not have the kind of communal centers we have in the West. Reverend Moon could legitimately say, "this is what I had in mind all along," even though he never talked about it in the United States because we had a different focus there. I think it is the demographic basis for the growth of the Church everywhere. The concept of home church is focused on service to our neighbors, not on evangelizing them, but people will logically be drawn to the Church, and more and more associate members will find their religious life there.

My wife was a missionary in Seoul for more than a year, and reported great progress in the home church program.

It is part and parcel of the conversion process of becoming a Moonie that your attitudes toward marriage become very positive, even if you had been lukewarm towards the idea of family. Obviously, there is a strong acceptance of celibacy among the members as brothers and sisters before marriage. This is a necessary and chaste preparation for the vocation of family life. At the very beginning I knew I was going to be matched by Reverend Moon, but I expected it was going to be a long way off, and rightly so because I wasn't ready. I think I caught the spiritual significance of marriage rather late when I heard an excellent lecture about our religious dispensation, that for us the form of divine grace is oriented toward family. It's a process of restoration. Human beings fell by a very definite process of motivations and events, and salvation means that we just have to reverse the course.

XV

GENEVIEVE — FAMILY TROUBLES

In France the State does not provide subventions for private schools and universities, so that during the summer, after I received my diploma from the lycee, I wanted to make some money to help me go to the Catholic University in the fall. I needed one more year of college preparation before I could begin to study in the medical school. It was always my wish to be useful to other people and to serve them; that's why I planned to be a doctor. So I decided to work in a hospital in Lyons, which was about twenty-five miles from my home village. I worked there four days a week and was living with an old lady who let me stay in her home, free of rent, because I took care of her, did her shopping, and sometimes even cooked meals.

The rest of the week I spent home with my family. Now, the last day I was home, which was a Tuesday evening, there was a program on television attacking sects and cults, as they were called. As I watched and listened to this program I thought to myself: How is it possible, if it is so bad, that some young people get attracted to these religious groups? I thought I should check this out for myself, and see what the truth is. I determined that night to go visit one of these cults and talk to the people there. I didn't know any of them, nor where I could find them.

Usually I took the afternoon bus back to my hospital work in Lyons, but the next day, for some reason, I decided to take the early morning bus. Two seats in front of me I overheard a young girl talking to an old lady about a new Christian group she had met. One of her remarks was that "they are a bit intellectual, but they live up to what they say." We both got off the bus at the same stop in the city. I felt a kind of strong urge to talk with her. "I heard what you said to that lady, and I would like to know the address of those people." She said, "Well, you know, yesterday was the first time I was there. I don't know much about them, but I'll give you the address." That same night I went there and found it was the Unification Church, but they called themselves "Pioneers of the New Age."

I was mainly trying to find out why such bad things were said about them on the radio and television. I did not think they could teach me anything about religion. So, when they started explaining their ideas to me I did not really have an open mind. I felt that I knew enough to teach them, and not to be taught by them. As a matter of fact, some of their basic ideas about the purpose of life seemed quite reasonable to me, but I responded with some counter-arguments. I guess they thought I was not interested in them, so they didn't invite me to come back. Afterwards, when I was on the street, I realized that I had not been courteous to them. I felt bad because I had been too proud. So, the next day I went back and apologized for being so rude, and said, "I really want to listen to what you have to say."

During the whole month of August, 1974, I went to see them whenever I had time off. An older couple was in charge of the center, but all the others were young men and women. I was very impressed with what I saw of the relationship between boys and girls. I belonged to Christian groups in my school and in my parish, but they had difficulty in doing things together. There was always the problem that some boys would go with some girls, and all the group activities failed because of that. The young people at the center never paired off like that. They lived in a community like a family, and they always said that God must be first in all human relationships.

That was my idea also, that God comes first in everything we do, but from early childhood I always had some questions about God. One point I questioned myself on was how could I become perfect. We are supposed to be sons and daughters of God, and when I told my grandmother that I wanted to be somebody good, and always good, she would remind me of Original Sin and tell me, "you cannot be perfect." I remember that when I was ten years old I had that call: from now on I'm going to be only good. But there was always some dispute with my two younger sisters, and I would fail to be good. When I was twelve I thought maybe it's not possible, but it will be when I get to be eighteen.

I had a special relationship with my grandparents, and they talked a lot to me about God, and I would open my heart to them. I needed to know what this Original Sin was so that I could stop doing it. They said you always have something bad in you, and that is written in the Bible. This is as difficult to understand as for a

camel to go through the needle's eye. I talked a little
bit with my parents about that, but not too much, and
less with my father who was a stern and strong Catholic.
There was also another thing about sin I couldn't
understand: that Jesus died because of our sins.   I
couldn't accept in my heart that God the Father sent His
son to death on earth.   I felt that Jesus wanted to do
something greater than that.   How can we say He saved
the world if this world is suffering so much today?   So
I felt there must be a better answer, but I didn't know
what.

Something was lacking in the explanations I was
given.   I was looking for better understanding from the
Marianist Brothers at school and from the religious
books we had at home.   My mother teaches religion, so we
had the books and I even read Teilhard de Chardin.   We
were a real Catholic family.   My mother's sister was a
nun, so was her aunt.   My father has a cousin who is a
bishop and another who was a Carmelite. Both my parents
came from large families; they were all very religious
people, but I never got to know them all.   As far as I
could know about them they didn't seem to have the same
struggles that I had with all these religious questions.

Three times during those years I went as a pilgrim
to Taize, which is a wonderful place for prayer and
meditation.   I liked what they were saying about the
love of God and that we children of God must love one
another and do good to everyone we meet.   I bought
several of their books, read them carefully, and I still
like them.   I kept asking questions, and I was searching
for the way to avoid sin and to achieve some kind of
perfection in the eyes of God.   The last time I went to

Taize it was very crowded, and I was put into a large
tent with many boys and girls. Among them there was no
talk at all of God, and I felt that the atmosphere was
very humanistic. Their behavior was a disappointment
for me.

Meanwhile, I was meeting as often as I could with
the people in the Unification community. In those days
we didn't have seminars or weekend workshops like we
have today. We had an old book that gave the basics of
Divine Principle, and the ones who knew it best
explained it to the rest of us. I didn't agree with
everything, especially the interpretation of history
through the centuries. The first part of Divine
Principle, about creation and the nature of God, could
also be taught in the Catholic schools. I felt that the
teaching about Original Sin and the fall of man was
exactly true. I saw now what it means to say that Jesus
was the Messiah and that the people failed to help Him
fulfill His mission.

One weekend in August, when I was home, I tried to
talk with my mother about these people I had met in
Lyons. I said, "you know mother, they are a nice
Christian group. They believe different from what you
were always teaching me, but really they are very good
young people, and I am sure you would like to meet
them." She said, "you have to be careful about the kind
of people you go with, especially if they are not
Catholics. We are well-known in this town, and people
will talk." I didn't say how deeply involved I was
getting with the group; and I didn't try to explain what
the teachings were. She found some reason or other for
not coming to visit. I could almost imagine she heard

the neighbors whispering: "we thought this was a good family. She is teaching religion and now look at what her daughter does." So, I didn't say anything more to her.

At the end of the summer I had to give up my job at the hospital. I went home to prepare for my next school year at the Catholic University. I wanted to study juvenile delinquency, and I took a very good course in pedagogy that was Christian-oriented. I liked that. I also joined with a Christian student group and went to several meetings. At the end of October we had a picnic out in the countryside with large numbers of university students. I tell you right now I was completely disappointed by what I saw, boys and girls flirting around, drinking too much wine, and getting into nasty quarrels. I don't want to say the whole Catholic Church is like that. I felt in my heart that God cannot call me to be there with them, but really called me to be with those people in the Unification Church. I wanted to go back there and listen more to what they had to say because I felt God is more present there than in this Christian student group.

I went home from the university on the first of November. Usually we go to visit my grandparents, my father's parents, in the south on France on All Saints' Day. I told my parents that I had to study and that I wanted to stay home alone, and they agreed. I spent the whole day walking in the countryside and talking with God. I didn't even stop to eat. I used to talk to God about everything, even if it was something not so good. I would say, "I feel bad about this, and I don't know what I should think. What do you think about that?" At the end of the day I felt that something was telling me - I did not hear any voice - "You go back there and look at what they have to say." I felt that if God wants me to be there, I would have to go, and never mind if my parents think it is wrong.

Back at the university in Lyons I took the first free evening I had to visit the center. I had a rented room in a students' residence hall, but I somehow felt drawn to join that group. I was fully aware that I was young, that there may be other groups in town, and that I could be making a mistake. So I told God, "I am completely sincere. I want to do this only for You. If I am doing something wrong please show me." I decided then that I would live in that center and work with them. The interesting thing is that they never invited me. No one ever witnessed to me. I myself asked them, "What is the condition if I want to join? Do I have to pay something? Do I have to sign anything?" All they said was that "if you would like to come with us, you must believe what we believe."

The first advice they gave me was that I must go back to my village and tell my parents of my decision. I should not do something behind their backs. I did not expect my parents to be pleased, but I was now strong in my resolution that I must do this. I knew that if my mother was against it my father would be twice as strongly opposed. Mother and daughter can most often understand each other. I wanted to tell them, but I could not find any easy way to do it, so I simply said: "I have something to tell you. I joined the Moonie group." That was like a bomb explosion. The reaction was as terrible as though I said I was pregnant.

Actually I didn't call them Moonies. They were the
"Pioneers of the New Age," but all my parents knew was
that they were a non-Catholic religious group. These
were heretics. If you are not a Catholic in France you
are a heretic, and if you are a heretic you go to hell.
What parents want their daughter to go to hell? When I
was a good student my parents had great hope for me, and
suddenly I got on the path to hell with the heretics.

They were both excited and upset, and they asked me
to talk with two priests who were close friends of the
family. One was the rector of the seminary for the
Oblates who have a long tradition in that part of
France. Then they called in another priest, the one who
had performed their marriage many years ago, and he
travelled many miles when they asked him to come talk
with me. These were very friendly and very learned men
who knew everything about Catholic theology, but had
never studied the <u>Divine</u> <u>Principle</u>. I suspect they
didn't take me seriously and thought this was just a
passing notion. For them the problem was that my
parents were getting so upset. They were saying, "you
should think about your parents." I was aware of that,
but I also knew that the call of God was stronger than
that. I respect and love my parents, but I cannot stay
home and love them if the world is crying out for help.
In the end what could the priests say except, "if you
think that is the way for you, well that's it, but try
to be careful."

Of course, I was not only changing my church
affiliation, but I was leaving home permanently. If I
had told them that I wanted to enter the convent, they
would have said that I must think carefully about that

and pray to know the will of God to be sure. Because of our ancestry it would not have been so shocking. Maybe, actually, they would have been proud. When I was a little girl - we were three sisters - my father often introduced us with the remark, "they are going to be nuns." I suppose my father could have wished that. Certainly, he would not have been so strongly against it. I wish they would have come along with me and said, "we'll go and check this out with you. If it is good, you can stay there. If it is bad you come back with us." But it was clear that we just couldn't discuss it. Now that I reflect about it maybe I could have spent more time with them, preparing them for it, discussing it for two months or so before becoming a member. But I wanted to be open and sincere, and actually thought that was the best way.

So I moved to the center in Lyons, but within the week, on a Friday night, my father came and took me back. He just knocked on the door and asked to see me, but the brother who opened the door did not know who he was, and let him walk in. He grabbed me and forced me outside. He was very strong, and I could not resist. I could have called the police, but my father is my father and I didn't want to make trouble for him. He was really mad and not in control of himself at all. I could have made a scene, but I didn't because my mother was in the car with him. I went home with them and behaved the way they wanted me to, knowing in my heart that if God wanted me to come back there would be a way to come back.

They wanted me to return to the University at Lyons; and that was also my intention. After a few days home - relatively peaceful because I did not argue with them - my father drove me back to the city. The next day I moved back into the center, but I continued my university studies for only about two weeks and then decided to cooperate full-time with the brothers and sisters there. Several of them were continuing their studies; one was studying to be a doctor. Some were employed and shared their income with the group. One man was working in a shoe company; one woman was a nurse; another was secretary to a doctor. The rest of us were fundraising in the streets. We were painting small cards, mainly houses and scenery, and selling them while we also witnessed to anybody who would stop and listen.

My parents and I did not communicate for a while, but I had the fear that my father may attempt again to get me out of the center. We prayed together in the group about this conflict and tension, and we concluded that I had better get away from Lyons for a while. I was only twenty-five miles from my home town, and the situation continued to be tense. I went to Strasbourg and lived with the members there, fundraising and witnessing. At New Year's in 1975, I joined the group in Paris. I went home for Easter to attempt a reconciliation with my family. I wanted to stay a few days and talk things over with them, but they would not listen. The only thing they could say was that I was in the wrong. All day long they said, "how could you do such a thing!" My mother was crying. My father got so angry he wouldn't talk to me. So I had to leave without having a quiet discussion with them.

In Europe, in those days, we didn't have the organized system of instruction that later developed in the Church. There were no weekend workshops, or seven-day seminars and retreats. In a sense there was nobody who felt capable of being the teacher for us. We learned from the book on <u>Divine</u> <u>Principle</u>, from each other in our conversations, and in our prayer. We were sure we had the true revelation from God, and we explained it the best way we could. While I was in France we organized the first international team, and travelled in the countries of Europe. During the next five years I went with them, fundraising and witnessing in France, Germany, Italy, and England.

My life as a member of the Church has been that of an itinerant worker and missionary. Even when I came to the United States I was always with a mobile team, sometimes with three members, sometimes as many as nine. We started in upstate New York, through Albany, Syracuse, Rochester, Buffalo, and then down to New York City. The members of the team often changed, but we were always international, and I think this was Reverend Moon's program: that we should represent a unification of all peoples. I got to know New Jersey from south to north, and witnessed in Maryland, Washington, Virginia, and South Carolina. Most recently I have worked in Boston and New England. Maybe it's a special mission to be an itinerant, and there are also other members who prefer this to a settled life at one of the centers.

I am more than satisfied with this way of life; I am happy that this is what God wants me to do. I have not had doubts about my vocation, but I wouldn't say that every day is a joyful experience and that there are no hardships. The antagonism against us seems to be worse in the United States than in Europe, and you suffer that when you are out on the streets witnessing and fundraising. Sometimes people say, "Moonie, get out of here." Others have shouted, "We're going to kill you Moonies." You're always confronting some form of hostility. Of course, if you have a mission to work in an office, or in one of our businesses, or you're going to graduate school, nobody bothers you. But if you are fundraising you face that every day.

My vocation to marriage was recognized in 1979 when Reverend Moon matched me with a wonderful brother who is an Irish-American and also came from a strong Catholic family background. We had a three-year period of separation and were then in the large wedding at Madison Square Garden in New York. During these years my father continued to be hostile to the church, made public charges that I had been deceived into joining and that I was being held captive in America. I corresponded with my parents with some regularity but had no answers from them until a cable arrived saying that my father was seriously ill. My husband and I flew back to visit him and were able to make a kind of reconciliation before he died. My mother and my sisters have now accepted me as a kind of prodigal daughter, and I don't think I can ask for more.

XVI

WALTER — PEACENIK FOR GOD

I was part of the love generation that spawned the free speech movement, the Students for a Democratic Society, the Jesus Movement in its many forms, and kept the civil rights movement alive and well. We were the heart of the anti-war movement in the late sixties. I was an undergraduate student at Princeton even before the Tonkin Resolution that got us into the French war in Viet Nam. That was the first time I went to prison. I was found guilty of resisting the draft as a conscientious objector. After six months in prison I went to continue my education at Berkeley, and participated in protests and demonstrations that put me back in prison for a year.

By the time I left Berkeley it was obvious that the United States would shortly have to get out of Viet Nam. The anti-war demonstrations reached their peak, with a quarter-million participants in the nation's capitol at the end of 1969, but the combat troops did not pull out of Viet Nam till three years later. Logically, the anti-war movement then had no place to go, but the students themselves had gradually become militant. The only people I knew in the peace movement who really had a vision of the future were the Marxists. I didn't like that vision because they were replacing our social problems with a system that promised to contain problems that were far worse. Perhaps I was an escapist because I literally headed for the hills. I went to the mountains of northern California, bought a small farm, grew a beard and long hair, and started reading the Bible.

That was the time of the new religious movement; college students and ex-students were very much a part of it. Gurus came out of the East and attracted large numbers. I had met some of them, and I read books about Buddhism and Hinduism, and also about American Indian religions. But I grew up Presbyterian, so I also had to read the Bible. My father and mother used to send me to Sunday school, but they rarely went to church services themselves. I was a churchgoer right on into college when students were dropping out of the conventional churches and taking up with all kinds of pseudo-mysticism. I had tried out the communes and had lived off and on with such groups, but I got away from it all in a cabin on my own land of twenty acres.

This got me away also from the common-law marriage I had contracted just after graduation from college. It was a friendly breakup with a woman who was deeply religious and later joined the Unification Church. There was a lot of work on the little farm, mainly growing vegetables, but I had time to walk around the hills, meditate about time and eternity, and I began to have spiritual experiences. It was nothing terribly dramatic, but there were periods when I really felt God's presence. I distinctly remember feeling that I was nothing more than a steward of this property. I was there to cultivate it for the real owner who created it and really owned all things on earth. I felt a responsibility for taking care of his property; and I could

see God's pain because of the way people in general
abuse and waste the earth that He gave us.

My first contact with the Unified Family was at
Oakland in 1973, when I visited the woman I had lived
with. She introduced me to Dr. Durst who had himself
just recently joined the movement. His was the first
lecture I heard in this group. I remember being
inspired by him but in a very diffuse kind of way. In
other words, the precise content of the lecture escapes
me, but I think it was much more about God's existence
and providence than it was about the teachings of
Reverend Moon. I specifically remember being baffled
afterward as to the main theme of his discourse. The
people I met at the Oakland center seemed very wholesome
and outgoing. I felt a good spirit there. I felt
embraced by God's love, so to speak, but at the time I
was interested in a lot of other religious movements.
In some ways I was getting close to the Divine Light
Mission and Guru Maharaj Ji. That was mainly because
some good friends of mine had recently joined him, but I
also met with Sufis and Vedantist people and evangelical
Christians.

Among the non-Christian youth religions the Divine
Light Mission emphasized meditation and a sort of
passive bliss. In fact, they often talked of their
members or premies as being "blissed out" on mediation,
and as far as I know they were not doing it on drugs. I
saw no hope in movements like that for being a force to
change society. What I was craving was a movement that,
like Marxism, had a vision and a discipline for changing
this world and the energy and the program to do it, but
was spiritual and not atheistic. My older sister was an

active member of the Communist Party, and continues to be. Later on, when I had more knowledge and experience, I must say that the Unification Church appealed to me on that basis. It turned out to be much more than a prayer group for personal salvation.

The charismatic Catholics were getting people to join them, but they were new at that time and pretty low key on the West Coast. I had had some contact with Catholics. As an undergraduate at Princeton I went to the Catholic services for a year. That was before I got drafted. So, from Oakland I went back up to my mountain retreat, but I came back into the city to hear Reverend Moon at the end of 1973. At this point the woman I had visited had gone somewhere else. I remember being shocked at Reverend Moon's mannerisms. He was sort of karate-chopping his way through the speech, and he was interpreted by Colonel Pak. I had never heard Korean before, especially the guttural type of language he pronounced. But I was impressed by the way he handled the crowd which was full of hecklers.

The speech was given at Sauerbach Hall on the Berkeley campus. It was a packed audience, and a lot of the students were hostile. One person stood up shouting something from the Bible, and someone else yelled at him about the exploitation of the masses. Reverend Moon managed to keep his composure through all of this, and even as one of these abusive people was being led out by the campus police for refusing to sit down and let the talk continue Reverend Moon said, "Let's give that man a round of applause for making the evening more memorable and exciting." I thought that was very well done. I was impressed also with the main theme of his speech which dealt with the contemporary crisis of Christianity in the western world. I looked on him as a preacher who was interpreting to us the Word of God.

No one among the members of the Unified Family there suggested that I join their movement. I think they were all pretty much laid back in those days, nothing pushy or aggressive about them. After the Moon lecture I went back up to my farm. I supplemented my income there with a part-time job in the local hospital. Six months later I decided to switch jobs, and I had a week off before the new job started. My twenty acres of land needed plenty of work and there was no shortage of things to do, but I needed a change. At that point I was seriously seeking God's will and praying to find out what He wanted me to do with the rest of my life. I got the crazy idea that I should again visit my old friend, the woman who had joined the Unified Family and was now living at a movement center in West Virginia.

It turned out that I had just enough money in the bank to buy a seven-day excursion plane ticket, round-trip, to Huntington, West Virginia, and have maybe twenty dollars left over. It was one of those special fares, so I couldn't come back earlier without paying more money, and I had no more money. Just before I took off I phoned the center to say I was coming to visit them. They were surprised that I would fly all the way from California just to stay a while at their center. My old friend with whom I wanted to talk had, meanwhile, been informed that she had been assigned to Barrytown for further training. The Church had just bought the Christian Brothers Scholasticate there and was using it for reeducation and training of seasoned members before opening it the following year as the seminary. She was not being reassigned because of my phone call. I did see her briefly at the airport. I was coming in, and she was going out. It was clear at that point that God wanted me there but not to see her.

This was not the way I had expected it to be, and I was stuck at the center for seven days. There was no way I could get out of there with this excursion ticket. They welcomed me and put me up for what turned out to be a one-man, seven-day workshop of Unification lectures. That was the first time I had heard an explanation of the Divine Principle. I remember the guy would finish every lecture by saying, "Do you have any questions?" I kept my mouth shut the whole time because I didn't have questions; I just had a lot of objections. In between these so-called lecture periods I helped out with carpentry in the health food store they were building.

On the last day working there I just told the brother it was about time for me to take off. I remember this distinctly because he came over and bought me a milkshake and said, "you can't go." I told him there is no question about it. I'm leaving. He said very quietly, "God wants you to stay." I was completely taken aback because I had been praying to God to tell me what he wanted of me. And here was a man telling me what God wanted. I suppose he was a charismatic person, and at that point I felt like he had the spirit of God within him. No one before in my whole experience of all these religious movements had just come right out and said, "God wants you to do something." I took this seriously, but I said, "I have to go back. I can't just abandon my farm and walk out on my employer. I'll tell you what.

I'll go out there, find a replacement for my job, give the farm over to somebody, and come back to West Virginia."

As the plane was climbing out of the airport I suddenly realized what I had promised. It was not as though I had rationally planned my future, but I always thought of myself as a person who kept his word. The brother back at the health food store didn't know that. He told me later that he thought he had lost me. I had also promised the people at the hospital to take the job as a medical laboratory technologist, for which I had been trained in the Army before going to prison. It took me several months to find a replacement for this part-time job. I was not sure that I should completely give up my equity in the farm, and I hedged my decision by handing over the cabin and land rent-free to a city couple who wanted to experiment with that style of life.

After making these arrangements I went back to Huntington and moved in provisionally. In other words, I did not become a member of either the center or the movement. I thought I'd stay for six months to see if God really wanted me there. At the end of that time I remember one night taking a long walk and wrestling in myself with the choice: should I stay, or should I leave? I mentally made lists of reasons for both options. Generally speaking, I was then sold on the truth of the Unification movement. I could go back and witness to Reverend Moon among my friends in the hills of northern California. I'd be a sort of John the Baptist figure for the Second Advent. Or I could stay here in West Virginia and sacrifice myself to the larger purpose of the Unified Family. so I laid out these two lists in my mind and presented them to God in prayer. The voice I heard inside of me favored the second option: that I stay with the Family.

This was a conversion process, but it was fairly complicated. There were several incidents in this calling from God. One was the call to go to West Virginia from California in the first place, and that seemed more impulsive than rational. The second call was the promise to return, which was triggered by the brother's statement about God's will for me. The third call was the decision to dedicate my life to God in this group. I think all three of them must be taken together. My commitment then also seemed somewhat complex. To some extent it was to the movement itself; to some extent to the teaching of the Principle; and to some extent to Reverend Moon, whom I hardly knew at that time. The major guiding force, I think, was this internal voice responding to my prayers.

The conditions of membership in the Unification Church have never been highly formalized, at least in my personal experience. One does not go through a public ceremony of initiation and acceptance. At that time there was a mimeographed membership form, a single sheet of paper. It asked name, address, educational background, and employment experiences. It asked whether you have any special skills. Another question was: "When did you accept the teachings of the Divine Principle?" I must confess that I never filled in that blank space because I was not sure. That's the only membership form I ever signed, and I've never been asked

since then whether I accept all the Principle. Obviously I accept a good deal of it, or I wouldn't have stuck
it out this long.

Whatever doctrinal doubts may have lingered in my
mind I was determined to plunge completely into the
program and the works of the movement. I joined with
the attitude of sacrificing everything. It was similar
to the attitude I had when I committed myself as a
conscientious objector to the war. I saw what I thought
I should do and I forgot everything else. This was true
also in relation to the universal vocation of
Unificationists to marriage and family life. I am sure
I knew from the beginning, in a cognitive way, that the
movement has True Parents and that the blessing of
marriage opened the channel of salvation. I didn't join
the church with anything like that motivation. I was
sure that was several years away. I couldn't think that
far ahead. I just thought I would plunge in and worry
about the future when I got around to it.

The fact is that I soon began witnessing to the
truths of Divine Principle in the urban areas of West
Virginia, but I needed to learn more about it. In
March, 1975, I was called to Barrytown for the first
120-day training session ever tried in the movement.
There were almost three hundred of us from all over the
country, and it included people who were to be sent out
as foreign missionaries. Half of us were being prepared
to be American missionaries, or pioneers as they were
then called. This was really an exciting event for me
because I was a relatively new member, and I listened
with deep interest to the stories of the veterans. The
workshop lectures were given by Mr. Ken Sudo, who had

long been a father figure on the West coast. I ended up getting sent first to Stamford, Connecticut and then to Burlington, Vermont where I spent one year as acting State director.

My State leadership in Vermont ended when we began preparations for the "God Bless America" Yankee Stadium Rally in June, 1976. Like everybody else, I helped out on that gigantic program. Right after that we had a big meeting of all the State leaders at Belvedere, East Garden actually. Father discussed leadership qualities and reassigned a lot of the leaders to different States. He believed in the circulation of talent, and no one was long enough at one position or in one place to get bored with it. Apparently Mr. Sudo, whom I got to know well during the training sessions, asked that I be appointed his assistant. So I went down with him to Washington to get ready for the Washington Monument Rally.

The opportunity for further study came when I was accepted at the Barrytown seminary to be in the class that started in September, 1976. In a scholarly way it opened up the whole world of comparative religions which I had only sampled with the sects and cults that had flourished among the college students. I got into religious history but especially into the great varieties of theological controversies and doctrines. I ended up dealing more with the theories of evolution, which is a throwback to my scientific studies as an undergraduate. This had important connotations in the light of the historical development of restoration and salvation described in the <u>Divine Principle</u>.

At the same time I saw the Unification movement as a strong force for social transformation. Moral corruption abounds not only in private life and in the midst of families, but also in public circles of business and politics. The large social structures are in need of reform, but they are secondary to the people within them. Even if we succeeded in correcting the structures they would be practically irrelevant if the people are morally rotten. We don't need to change the American electoral system for some other political system, but let's make sure that the system we've got is being used for God's purpose. Unlike the Marxists, I don't think there is anything fundamentally wrong with big business as a structure. Our problem is with the morality of the people involved in all these structures.

At the level of everyday life I see the greatest hope, I guess, in our continuing emphasis on home church. I had the honor of being in the seminary graduating class of 1978 when we initiated home church in Britain. The general concept of home church is that each member makes a fairly limited neighborhood his or her home, and takes responsibility to be of service to the people living in the surrounding 360 households. This, I think, is actually the key to transforming society, to develop small healthy God-centered neighborhoods where people are concerned about family and childraising, morality and physical needs like street-cleaning and food distribution. I see that as a really practical grassroots approach to the restoration of the Kingdom of God on earth. The Divine Principle is interpreted systematically as the development of stages, or circles, from individual to family to community to nation to world. I don't expect the Kingdom to be completely here before my grandchildren arrive on the scene, but I am hoping that the worst of the job will have been finished by that time.

If we have enough of these small moral and spiritual communities that have a positive influence on society, in the long run they are going to mean reform of the whole society. I won't say that that alone will do it, but I see that as the most necessary and, in some ways, most difficult job. In the military we used to say you can have all the fancy artillery and enormous bombers, but you ultimately win the war with the infantry on the ground. I don't want to push that analogy too literally, because in our movement we also try to influence businessmen and politicians and scholars and the people in power everywhere. The movement is trying to reach people at all levels, but I still see the grassroots approach as the part that ultimately gains the victory on a permanent basis.

XVII

DOROTHY — MATURE PROFESSOR

My Catholic friends who are Moonies tell me that I am a delayed vocation to the Unification Church. That means that I'm about a dozen years older than the average American recruit is when coming into the Church. I graduated from Wellesley, then did graduate work in modern languages at Vanderbilt University, where I married a fellow student in 1972 and got my doctorate degree. My husband had a fellowship in Brazil, and I went along to learn Portuguese. The marriage didn't work because I was not really interested in it, and we had an amicable divorce after three years.

My parents were highly educated professional people who raised me and my brother to be good Episcopalians. We went to Sunday school and communion classes and did actually learn something about the Bible. I studied religion for one semester in college, but didn't do so well. I considered myself a devout member of the episcopal Church, but I don't think I ever had a personal relationship to God. I went to church regularly and took the sacraments. I was confirmed and married in the church. The man I married wasn't particularly religious. He thought he was too intelligent to take God and religion and church seriously. At that point in my life I can't say that I paid much attention to religion either.

Maybe that's why I never heard of Reverend Moon or
his religious movement before October, 1978. I used to
read the newspapers and some news magazines, but I don't
know why I never noticed the bad press that Reverend
Moon was getting. I had a post-doctoral fellowship at
Columbia University that year and was living in
Greenwich Village. One day I happened to meet a young
German guy who was distributing leaflets for the World
of Hope Festival. There was no rational motive why I
should attend but I did, and I got interested in the
weekly programs at the Unification Center. What moved
me the most was the tremendous amount of effort the
members put into these events. They included the New
Hope Singers, the Korean dancers, films and testimonies,
and every week a lecture on one chapter of Divine
Principle by Bo Hi Pak, who is Reverend Moon's chief aid
and interpreter.

The lectures sounded interesting so I got a copy of
Divine Principle, but I wasn't at all impressed with the
translation or the grammar. I thought some if its
theories were more psychological than theological. I
began to read outside critics who made charges of
Gnosticism and Pelagianism against it. When I looked at
the book as a whole I realized that it was internally
very coherent. It began to make sense to me as a total
entity. I was getting more curious about this religion,
so I attended a two-day workshop which I didn't
particularly like because I had a lot of questions that
were not being answered.

I guess it was a mistake to try to do this on my
own. I was determined not to be manipulated by anybody,
and I deliberately avoided getting overfriendly with any

of the members. Maybe that's a kind of intellectual pride that goes with higher education. I let it be known that I would not join the Church, so nobody ever asked me to do so. I wanted to think this out by myself. I had come to see that the <u>Divine</u> <u>Principle</u> had a kind of inner logic. As an Episcopalian I could agree with the ideas in it, which seemed to me to be basic Christianity with an added dimension. This is what they called the completed new testament, a new revelation, a new way of explaining the Christian tradition. I decided to attend a seven-day workshop directed by Reverend David Hose, who proved to be a very clear lecturer and a wonderful personal counselor.

Under his guidance I examined my life style and for the first time in my life began to ask serious questions about personal morality. I think this was the critical point of my religious conversion. I realized that certain things should change, especially in the man-woman relationships. I used to think that original sin was just something that happened in the beginning of human history, but now I knew that every time people have sex outside of marriage they are committing the original sin. When I told my lover that we could be friends and nothing more he was enraged and threatening. I was very scared, but I kept my resolve to have only pure relationships. I didn't drink so much, just a glass of wine now and then. Internally, I guess, I decided to become a better person.

There were many personal implications in the teachings of <u>Divine</u> <u>Principle</u>, and I asked many questions that I wanted to clarify. I wanted to make sure that I was going in the right direction. During

the early months of 1979 I got a great deal of explanations from Reverend Hose and his staff at the center.   I
finally told him, "this is great.   I approve of this
life style, but I'm not ready yet to join full-time."
Nevertheless, I felt that I could accept the teachings
of the Church, the interpretation of God's relations to
humanity, and also the moral life style that was expected of members.   I decided to become a home member, that
is, an associate who believes in the Principle, follows
the ideals and practices of the Church, but does not
make the total commitment.

While I was spending that year in New York on a
fellowship grant from the National Endowment for the
Humanities, I was also really between jobs.   I applied
for positions in several universities, and I was
accepted on the faculty of modern languages at Christian
Brothers' College in Memphis.   I had no qualms of
conscience in taking this job because I knew I would
continue to lead a moral and prayerful life.   I spent
the academic year at Memphis where the Moonies had an
apartment for a fundraising team, but I had no contact
with them.   On a couple of trips home to the East I went
to some Unification Church holidays, saw a few friends,
but otherwise during that year I was almost completely
by myself, which was great.

Up to that point I was not really aware of the vast
wave of negative publicity about Reverend Moon and the
Church.   I read everything negative I could get my hands
on, especially books about former Unificationists like
Edward, Crazy for God, the Underwoods, Hostage to
Heaven, and Stoner and Parke, All God's Children.   In
these books I wanted to determine why some people left

the Church. I thought I discovered that none of them said anything bad about the Divine Principle or about the goals and ideals of the movement. In other words, they seemed to quit mainly for subjective and personal reasons. They complained that others did not live up to the standards of the Church, or that they found it too difficult. Since that time I have talked with some ex-members who said, "I just couldn't take fundraising. I wanted to get married. I was tired. I wanted to have some money of my own." These people appreciated the ideals of the movement but thought they were not strong enough personally to fulfill those ideals.

In spite of all the negative books and stories, I realized that it was up to me as an individual to try. I had to do my share not only in my personal life but to help restore the world to God. When I was home on a visit in January, 1980, the Russians invaded Afghanistan. The teaching of the Unification movement recognizes the monstrous evils of Communism, and when that happened I suddenly appreciated the truth of what Reverend Moon was saying about this time in history. We are experiencing a most violent period of time, in some ways a turning point of good and evil. This communist invasion exemplified that teaching. I really felt convinced that in order to help on a larger scale it was not enough for me to be a good professor,but that I had to join the movement as a full-time member.

As I now understand Divine Principle, the world is at a crossroads of good and evil. A certain number of years are necessary to pay what we call indemnity, to pay for mankind's historical failures. Every time a person fails to fulfill his or her mission God has to start over again by choosing another individual, but the accumulated history behind that person has to be redone. That's why certain lengthy historical periods are necessary, when people must remain faithful before God feels they are ready to receive a new leader. We believe we are now at the point in time, approaching the end of the world. These are the last days. Because we are now two thousand years after Jesus, God finds it appropriate to send a new Messiah, a new Adam, a new champion, to create the Kingdom of heaven on earth.

My reading was extensive and my convictions grew stronger while I did my academic work at Memphis. I knew then that the movement was to be my life's vocation, and I called up Reverend Hose and told him I wanted to go to the Unification seminary. Then, without even receiving an application in the mail, I gave notice to the college dean that I would not renew my contract for the coming year. After my teaching year was over, in June 1980, I made a formal commitment as a full-time member of the Unification movement. I was given permission to spend three weeks with my mother in Connecticut and to straighten out my personal affairs.

Even though I had fully made up my mind I did a lot of deep meditation, of absolutely desperate prayer with God, and I cried a lot. I had to reinforce myself with the pragmatic conclusion that if the <u>Divine</u> <u>Principle</u> was true I had to go through with it. The teaching is that it is easier and more necessary to perfect oneself while one is physically here on earth. I believed that if it isn't done on earth it is very much harder in the afterlife. This was going to be a new and very different life style, and I was strengthening my mind and my heart to get on with it.

The pace began to pick up that first summer. I attended a three-week workshop for seminary candidates, where I met with a select group of experienced members from around the country. Not all of them were accepted for the seminary, but my early intuition about myself was absolutely correct when I was chosen. During the rest of the summer I worked with CARP, recruiting actively on the streets of New York, inviting young people to join the Church. As a new convert I thought I knew a lot about the Church, but I was a novice at witnessing to others. That was very difficult and even frustrating. New York is a tough town, and people are very cynical about religion.

I really did not know anything about the Church organization, and I was not used to working with a team. We kept at it for hours on end, and I learned to adjust myself and to live each day with incredibly demanding physical schedules. Inviting people to dinner and a lecture at the center required a gift of persuasion, but winning a new member was a real victory. I did manage to bring in one spiritual son, a student at Columbia University. He had not heard much about the church, but had a very open heart and was ready to embrace the teachings of religion. He later went to work with CARP down in Maryland. I want to emphasize that witnessing to our beliefs was our primary mission, and we did not expect all our hearers to join the Church.

In late December, when I had been a full-time member for only six months and was studying at the

Barrytown seminary, I was invited to a matching. By that time I was already thirty-five years of age, but I guess they thought I could handle it. Physically, of course, it was the right time and perhaps a little later than usual to get married, but spiritually I wasn't ready at all. I just couldn't go and present myself to Reverend Moon. The next matching was in June of 1982, and I had prayed a great deal in the intervening time to prepare myself. I had the strong thought that I believed was from God, that I should be matched with a Korean, but I was willing to accept the decision of Reverend Moon as coming from God.

We believe that God works through Reverend Moon, who can see a person's ancestry, but he doesn't know the specific details about the individual member, which is why he asks questions. During the matching he would walk up and down between the brothers and sisters. He stopped by me and asked, "Ph. D., how old are you?" When I told him he said, "Oh, so old. What can I do?" So three times he stood up all the brothers over thirty, but he couldn't find one for me who was a college graduate. Near the end of the matching he spotted this man who had been a member for five years, had not finished college but was a successful gemologist.

When Reverend Moon matches a couple he first sends them out of the room to talk it over. This boy and I took longer than usual; we talked for over an hour about all the very important things, our beliefs and expectations, and he was very honest with me. He told me right away that he was very attracted to a girl who was not a member of the Church. He had come to ask Reverend Moon to match him with this non-member, but now he thought it

may be God's will that he marry me. So, we went back
into the ballroom, bowed in acceptance to Reverend Moon
and went through the Holy Wine ceremony. This matching
took place in preparation for the mass wedding at
Madison Square Garden on July 1, 1982. Three days
before this event he phoned me and said, "I'm very
sorry, but I can't go through with it." He said he
loved this other girl enough to marry her, even if it
meant leaving the Church.

That was not too great a disappointment to me. I
had thought all along that it was God's will for me to
marry a Korean. I was occupied the rest of the summer,
going around the world with our Youth Seminar in World
Religions. I acted as counsellor and interpreter for
these young people who were guests of the Unification
movement. Then the call went out for a matching to take
place in Korea in October. I was very excited because I
felt that this time I would be matched with a Korean.
In our Church we have a belief that if you do your best
and you do not succeed you will receive a greater
blessing the next time. Perhaps I was a bit arrogant
when I said to myself: "Obviously I have to get a
Korean this time because I did my best the last time."

The matching ceremony in Seoul, Korea, took place
on three successive days. I had told Reverend Moon that
I wanted a Korean husband, so on the first day he asked
how many Korean men would volunteer for Western wives,
but there were only five who stood up. He looked them
over and decided that none of them was suitable for me.
He is actually slow to match Korean men with Western
women because they tend to be domineering and aggressive
toward women. He feels that Western men and Oriental

women are a better match and are likely to have a more successful marriage.

On the second day of the matching, the President of our seminary, Reverend David Kim, reminded Reverend Moon that I was willing to have a Korean husband, as if he didn't already know. He looked over at the Korean brothers and found no one for me. He came over and spoke to me in English, "No Koreans for you; and tomorrow I don't know." He patted me on the head in front of everybody. This is considered a great honor when Reverend Moon speaks to you personally, or pats you affectionately. Then he had the other seminarians line up, those who were waiting to be matched. He praised the seminary, said that he put great trust in us and that we would be the leadership of the Church in the future. He then stood up all the European brothers and then matched the seminary sisters one by one to a European. He skipped me, apparently deliberately, for which I was glad.

On the third day a large number of Korean brothers showed up for the matching. Their presence in such numbers was explained by the fact that most of them have regular jobs and do not live in centers as we do in Japan and in America. They worked in various parts of the country, and this was the day they could get off from work. Reverend Moon started with other groups. First, he talked to the African men and berated them for not bringing enough African women to be matched. He told them, "your heritage is one of laziness and promis- cuity, but we can start on the restoration by having blessed families with Oriental women or with Western women." Then he went to the Japanese whom he loves and

praises because they are so faithful. He then spoke to
the Korean sisters and brothers in their native
language, and seemed to be saying harsh things that I
did not understand. Then he came to the Western sisters
and gave a big speech about loving your own country.
Actually, it was directed at me. He said, for example,
"if an American sister wants to marry a Korean brother
because she doesn't like American men, that's a bad
attitude."

He smiled at me in a very friendly way, but I was
very confused and wondered whether God was telling me
through Reverend Moon that I should get over my
insistence on marrying a Korean. It was at this moment
that I conceded and prayed, "Well, God, if you want me
to work with some other professor who is American or
European, I guess I have to do it." Then Reverend Moon
had all the Western sisters stand up, and he started
matching. I was the first one, and we had a long
procession from one end of the room to the other, where
the Korean men were sitting. Reverend Moon was first,
then Colonel Pak and myself, Mr. Kim and Reverend Kwak
behind me. I did not feel excited or anxious. I just
felt completely calm and very trusting. Reverend Moon
talked to several Korean men, asked if they were over
thirty and what education they had. Finally, he reached
over and took one man by the arm and brought him over to
me, and said very gently in English, "This is the best
one."

We went out of the room to talk about whether we
should get married, and the conversation had to be
through an Austrian sister who interpreted for us. He
had been in the Church more than ten years, had brought

two spiritual children into the movement, and came to this matching in search of a Korean wife. He was completely in shock at first, at the idea of a Western wife. Koreans seem to be very earthy people. He was almost as old as I, and felt free to ask how many children I could have. I was so embarrassed. I had just met this man and to talk about having children with him. We talked about his home, which is in Inchon where MacArthur landed, and about the law office in which he is a partner. He is also into politics on the national level. The Holy Wine ceremony, in which we were solemnly matched for all eternity, was only a few days before the mass wedding at the Chomsu Gymnasium. This was on 14 October, which is a very significant church date for us. It was the day on which Reverend Moon was liberated from the communist prison camp by United Nations soldiers.

I returned to the seminary to teach, as well as to study more deeply the teachings of Divine Principle, and will probably go to Korea to live there next summer. This will not bother me at all. I lived in Brazil for three years, and one year in France. I want to learn Korean anyway, and have already started studying it, because Reverend Moon has been threatening for years to speak without a translator. It will be a different life style, but I've already ascertained that I could probably teach English and French at the University there. Since there are few centers of the kind we have in the States I will certainly be involved in home church and perhaps in both the International Christian Professors, Association and the Professors, World Peace Academy.

The next step in my vocation as a Moonie is to get started on my family. It is church practice to have a period of separation for as long as three years and then forty days more before consummating the marriage. When I get back to Korea I'll be almost thirty-eight, and I cannot wait forever to have children. I suspect that when I go there we'll wait another forty days, or will get an exception, since I will have been away from October to July; and that may be a long enough period of waiting. The fact is that Reverend Moon has made numerous exceptions for wives who are in their thirties, at the time of wedding. We shall, of course, abide by his decision and thus be obedient to the will of God.

XVIII

MARK — RATIONAL ANARCHIST

When I was twelve years old I made a conscious decision that I would not go through with Confirmation, although I had attended all the Catechism classes in Sunday school to get ready for it. My mother didn't seem to mind that. I'm not sure I told her my decision. We were nine children in the family; I was the second son and the fourth child. My father never went to Mass. My mother would go to Church with the kids and try to make it a serious commitment for herself and for us. Each one of us actually went through a stage when we wanted to go to Mass every Sunday. What happened to me is that I really liked studying the Catechism. But when I was in the Boy Scouts I went to a Methodist service one time, and a friend of mine who was an altar boy told me that's like going to Mass in the wrong church, and that was a mortal sin.

We lived in Highland, New York, and belonged to St. Augustine's Parish. My older brothers and sisters went to the parochial school there, but my father took them out because they didn't have a good sports program. He felt that sports was a very definite need in education if the child is to have a well-rounded character. I'm sure he thought that was more important than learning about religion, and he never talked with us about God and religion. All the children, one by one, dropped out of the church in their early teens, but I continued to believe in God in my own way. Basically, I figured that if there was a God, He was the creator of the world. If

He was the creator of the world then all people were His children. If God was the God of love, as they taught us in the Catechism, He could never condemn His children to hell, even for a mortal sin.

We moved to Marlboro where I went to public high school, and I breezed through fairly easily without applying myself to much study. It was a very small town, and there were only six hundred students in the entire school. It seemed that everybody was related to everybody else except us. I didn't have a broad base of relationship with the students in my school. They all struggled so hard with just the practical stuff of education that was so easy for me. There was, I'm sure, some intellectual arrogance on my part. I rationalized the situation by saying that they were "a bunch of fools." I also disapproved of their morality. Even the high school kinds were getting drunk and sleeping around, as they called it, and I didn't want to relate on that level. I don't know why, but no one was thinking the way I was.

Those were the years of the so-called youth revolution, and even the kids in high school were getting into the act of "demanding our rights." I read a lot about politics and government, and I thought that some day I would run for high political office and get into the government at Washington. I came to the conclusion that the American political system was much too large and complicated. I did not want to abolish the system like a destructive anarchist, but to simplify it. So I called myself a rational anarchist. I became a student of the Bill of Rights, with an emphasis on the right to assemble peaceably and to petition for the redress of grievances. My rational anarchism really insisted that society is organized for the benefit of the people, and that people are much more important than institutions.

Looking back from the perspective of the <u>Divine Principle</u> I think I was strongly influenced by the way my family lived. My parents loved each other – they still do – and the family always got together for dinner. We'd wait for my father to come home for dinner. At that time he worked in the city as a computer programmer for a Life Insurance company, and he would get home at seven o'clock. If he was coming home on a later train we all waited for him. I can now really appreciate my father's conscientious sacrifice for his family. At that time I didn't. I thought he should be around more so we could play football or baseball with him.

When I graduated from high school in 1973 my father wanted me to go to college, but I felt a fear of college because I knew that it was going to take a lot more work than I did to get through high school. My father had graduated from Wesleyan Connecticut and kept pressing me to continue my schooling. Instead, I got a job away from home as a shoe salesman. I wasn't making a lot of money, but I was very happy with what I was doing. Outside the store I was relating well with some people, but I also ran into the same kind of immoral element I had disliked in high school. Without any church motivation I resolved to be different. I said, "I'm going to be chaste. I'm not going to sleep around. I'm not going to get drunk, or lie or steal."

After four years of working at a variety of jobs I

gave in to my father's insistence. I enrolled at the State University of New Paltz. I really didn't want to go, but I did to satisfy him. I was a kind of fanatic about it and took twelve credit hours in a summer session in which you are only supposed to take nine hours. It was too much and I didn't have enough desire, so I failed every course except one in which I got an incomplete. My father was a pretty strict guy, and I was never able to tell him that I failed. In the next semester I enrolled again and this time I took out a loan. I was very dissatisfied with the professors, except the one who taught political science. The only course I passed - which I hardly ever attended - was a speech class called inter-personal communication, taught by a professor who was completely stoned out of his mind most of the time.

So, it was back to work. I had gone through a couple of cycles of different jobs, and I was working again as a salesman in a large department store. I wondered if this was where I would wind up. I didn't feel any problem with it as long as I could be happy there, but I wasn't. I still didn't have any real relationships. The only friends I had were friendly when they needed something I could do for them. This became the low point of my life, when I threw away my moral principles. I began drinking very heavily, and for a while I got into drugs. Because of that I began to slip badly on the job. I couldn't really perform as well as I should. Then I met a very religious girl who represented the standard of what I really wanted to be.

Sheila was admirable for her beauty, her strength

and her purity. She worked there in the same store, and
she did not hesitate to declare herself a Christian. I
started thinking again what I was going to do about
getting married and having a family where I could be
happy. I realized that a lot of myself was like my
father, and I didn't want to treat children the way I
had been treated. Here I was twenty-two, and I hadn't
been going to church for ten years, and in talking with
her I began to recognize that the thing that was missing
in my life was God. All along, when I talked with
people, if someone mentioned God I would just pull out
of the discussion. Here was a woman who affirmed, "Yes,
God does exist." I recognized in talking with her that
God had actually been present, speaking to me at
different times in the past.

As a matter of fact, she was witnessing her faith
to me in a very pleasant and charming way. She was
trying to get me to convert to Calvinism, but I didn't
think I would like being a Calvinist. I was
contemplating pulling myself together and going to
church with this wonderful girl, but I figured that I
couldn't be predestined if I had to respond to her
testimony. I was driving home one time and had an
experience like a vision, of sitting in a room with this
girl and with another spiritual being who didn't have a
descriptive self. I said that if we get married then
somewhere down the road one of us would die, and if we
had different concepts of God we would wind up in
different places. I said, "there would be no way to
find an absolute unity, harmony and love if you believe
in Christianity, and I simply believe that God is a
Father who wants His children to do good."

There was another spiritual experience that really shook me. I was attending the funeral of a distant relative, a good Catholic woman whom I knew mainly by reputation. For the first time in years I prayed for some sign that this person hadn't spent her life, in all this religious worship, in vain. There was a sign that came, and it was very dramatic. It was a real physical experience at that funeral. The sky had been gray for several days, as it gets in November in New York. There was a very cold wind at the grave site, and all of a sudden a bolt of lightning with no thunder. The skies actually opened, and it became a very bright day for about ten minutes. People made comments about it, saying that "she has been received into heaven." My own assessment then was that she hadn't really wasted her life with all that religion.

I had the feeling that life was closing in on me. I was trapped. I couldn't be me, because the people I associated with were so different from me. They were puzzled that I did not have sexual relations with any of the available girls, and there were some hints that I was a homosexual. That is really a powerful accusation in a he-man's world. I decided to get away from the New York scene and get a job as a scuba-diver teacher out in California. I got rid of my possessions, except what I could pack into three duffle bags, bought a fifty-five dollar bus pass and headed for the West Coast.

When I got to San Francisco I tried to contact my cousin, but failed. By some incredible circumstances, which I now believe was the hand of God, she was not at home. She was working an emergency night shift till three in the morning for IBM. She said it never happened before, and it never happened again. I camped out on a hillside in San Francisco, just rolled out my sleeping bag and crawled in. My cousin lived in one of those security apartment houses and apparently slept late the next morning, so I could not arouse her. I decided to venture into the city, and was immediately impressed how friendly the people were. In New York you can walk down the street and nobody knows you're there, but in California people look at you, they smile and say hullo. This is just anybody, everybody, and I met four or five good people.

I also had the address of a friend who lived in Berkeley, so I took the transit line over there. As I came out of the train station this person was standing halfway across the plaza. Our eyes met. She walked towards me, and I walked towards her, and we both said hullo at the same time. I felt that she was someone I knew, although I was sure that I had not physically met her before. She said her name was Christina, and I learned later that she was one of the earliest members of the Oakland Unification center. In some ways she seemed to be a clairvoyant. She knew that I was from a large family, that I had worked as a salesman, that I had goofed out of college. In our very pleasant conversation she told me she was with the Creative Community Project and that they had this ranch where they did organic gardening. This turned out to be the Boonville which has since then got a lot of publicity.

This was the first direct contact I had with a member of the Unified Family, the Unification Church, but not the first I had heard of them. My family lived right across the Hudson River from Barrytown, where they established the seminary in 1975. One of the places where I worked had a service contract with Bard College in Annandale. When Reverend Moon was arrested at the College I remember that the service manager complained about him and the Koreans. I remember also conversations I had with my mother about the Oakland Five who had been put in conservatorship in California. She said there is no such thing as brainwashing. If you raise your children well enough to make their own decisions you have to trust them do do what they think is right.

It was December, 1977, when I accepted the invitation to Boonville, where the talk was mainly about living on the land in harmony with nature. The people there didn't seem very religious in their conversation. There was nothing like a workshop, or a seminar, about the Divine Principle. Actually, I liked the idea of being on a farm where I could work and plant some vegetables. It was good to get away from the push of city living. They asked me to stay on, which I did without any urging from anybody. There was a group of people at the farm who were concerned about getting into harmony with each other and with the whole of nature, but there wasn't any talk about the Church.

After a week or so they asked me if I wanted to come to a workshop at their center in Berkeley. Here they were up front about the teachings of the Divine Principle, which were not introduced as the Unification teachings of Reverend Sun Myung Moon. I didn't ask any questions about that, and I don't think it would have made any difference if they did say this was his. This was the Unified Family working on the Creative Community Project. That was good enough for me, because I was

having a lot of experience of God during the week. I
had a feeling that I had arrived home at last. One
effect was that I stopped smoking cigarettes abruptly,
and I haven't had the urge to smoke since then. I had
been smoking marijuana and actually had some with me
when I came to California. I just poured it into the
river.

As I became better acquainted with the members of
the community I felt very wholesome that things were
going to work out for me. I went out with them on a
Friday night to Camp Kay, for a seven-day workshop. I
listened carefully to everything that was said about
God's creation of the world, and especially the story of
the Fall of mankind. I just listened and didn't ask
questions, and I found out later that they were worried
about me. They thought I was a very cold person. Perhaps I was, but I thought of myself as older and more
experienced than the other people on the workshop.
Probably I wasn't, but they just seemed younger. So, I
went through the seven-day workshop three times. I
believed that I could follow these teachings, even
though I did not fully understand them.

It came to me that the Fall of Man had to be interpreted in the context that we are all children of God.
I believed it meant that love has to be unselfish, that
you just don't have the love between a man and a woman
all by themselves, but that love has to be shared with
many partners. I felt that it should embrace me in a
separate way, because I was still looking forward to a
monogamous family life for myself. It took me a while
to understand that the concept of the Unified Family was
really a preparation for the blessing of the monogamous

couple and their children. I thought the <u>Divine Principle</u> was all-embracing, but one day I just woke up and it dawned on me that "that's what they are talking about."

By the time I had gone through the advanced seminars on the Unification system I realized that this was for me, and I made up my mind that I wanted to join the movement permanently. It is interesting that they introduced Reverend Moon simply as the person who wrote the book we were studying. I had the impression that they didn't want to claim too much for him. I have since decided very definitely that he is the Messiah. That's my own personal belief. There are people who have been in the Church three or four years who won't say that. They don't know whether to believe it or not, but for myself it's true.

Of course, I've heard different interpretations of the mission of Reverend Moon. He himself spoke about playing the role of John the Baptist in preparation for the coming of Christ, the second advent. At another point he is the prophetic voice speaking in the name of God as the great historical prophets have done. He told Professor Richardson that everyone is a Messiah who does God's will. I define the Messiah as the person who is prodding me and bringing me to the fulfillment of my purpose. In that sense, I think that the girl back in New York who tried to introduce me to Calvinist thought was like a Messiah. In a very real way Messiahship fits the role of the spiritual parent, and the girl who first met me in Berkeley is my spiritual mother.

The more I learned about Reverend Moon the more I realized that he is a person who completely dedicates his entire life - all of his energies - to the accomplishment of God's will. He is not just leading this or that person to do the will of God, but his whole life and everything he does or has is dedicated to God. I don't want to suggest that he just decided one day to become the Messiah. I am sure he was sent by God with a mission. He was chosen by God. I think that Reverend Moon had the characteristics that God needed in putting his message across, the kind of person God could use, and Reverend Moon responded to the call.

I stayed in California for approximately five months, and was then assigned to New York to join one of the fundraising teams. That's what I've been doing since the summer of 1978, which meant a lot of travelling up and down the Eastern States. It is almost inevitable in this kind of work that you do some witnessing, which means explaining to people what you are trying to do in the service of God. Sometimes it's discouraging when people just turn away from you, or when they insult you, or even when they argue with you and refuse to accept the love of God in their lives.

In my thorough commitment to the Unification Church I realized that I could go back to my adolescent concept of being a rational anarchist. This means that I respect people without impinging on them. This was a development of the responsibility of a rational anarchistic society, because the Divine Principle demanded a thorough understanding of the need for service. I had learned the extreme importance of serving people, caring for their needs, fostering their spiritual life and development.

INDEX

STUDIES IN RELIGION AND SOCIETY